Stratified Policing

An Organizational Model for Proactive Crime Reduction and Accountability

Roberto G. Santos, PhD
and
Rachel B. Santos, PhD

ROWMAN & LITTLEFIELD
Lanham • Boulder • New York • London

Published by Rowman & Littlefield
A wholly owned subsidary of The Rowman & Littlefield Publishing Group, Inc.
4501 Forbes Boulevard, Suite 200, Lanham, Maryland 20706
www.rowman.com

6 Tinworth Street, London, SE11 5AL, United Kingdom

British Library Cataloguing in Publication Information Available

Library of Congress Cataloging-in-Publication Data

Names: Santos, Roberto, author. | Santos, Rachel Boba, author.
Title: Stratified policing : an organizational model for proactive crime
  reduction and accountability / Roberto Santos and Rachel Santos.
Description: Lanham, Maryland : Rowman & Littlefield, [2020] | Includes
  bibliographical references and index.
Identifiers: LCCN 2020031763 (print) | LCCN 2020031764 (ebook) | ISBN
  9781538126561 (paperback) | ISBN 9781538126578 (epub)
Subjects: LCSH: Crime prevention. | Police. | Problem solving.
Classification: LCC HV7431 .S257 2020 (print) | LCC HV7431 (ebook) | DDC
  363.2/3—dc23
LC record available at https://lccn.loc.gov/2020031763
LC ebook record available at https://lccn.loc.gov/2020031764

PRAISE FOR *STRATIFIED POLICING*

"I have had the honor of working directly with Dr. Roberto Santos and Dr. Rachel Santos for more than a decade. Their combined contributions to the development of essential and effective crime analysis practices to guide the deployment of police and community resources in rapid response to emerging crime patterns as well as to solve difficult crime problems, all supported by an accountability structure within police organizations, has been a major contribution to the fields of modern policing and crime prevention. This book should be on the desk of all law enforcement professionals dedicated to improving public safety by reducing crime and its harm."
—**Richard S. Biehl, director and chief of police, Dayton, Ohio**

"Read this book. When I found stratified policing, I was looking for something foundational to bring crime reduction, community engagement, and account-ability into the daily business of a police department. Working with Roberto and Rachel, we crafted a model of stratified policing that works specifically for my department. We have experienced substantial reductions in crime and continue to do so while having a community that supports our efforts. If you want a blueprint for effectively integrating evidence-based practices in your agency, this is it."
—**Scott C. Booth, chief of police, Danville, Virginia**

"What the authors have articulated in this book is an evidence-based approach to crime reduction that capitalizes on measurable outcomes. By empowering all levels of an organization with the responsibility, and frankly the motivation to become engaged, we see significant improvements in individual law enforce-ment officer performance. The Stratified Policing approach provides a significant return on investment. The Walton County Sheriff's Office is consistently recog-nized for our success in crime reduction which can largely be attributed to our adherence to the Stratified Policing model developed by the authors."
—**Michael Adkinson, sheriff, Walton County, Florida**

"The Stratified Policing model has proven to be effective in a statewide police agency. The flexibility of the model has allowed troop commanders of each region to draw from proven evidence-based approaches to shape and modify their policing strategies to meet the needs of their community. *Stratified Polic-ing* provides clear processes that have helped the Delaware State Police achieve significant reductions in crime while maintaining a strong positive relationship with the community."
—**Nathaniel McQueen Jr., secretary of the Department of Safety and Home-land Security, State of Delaware and retired Delaware State Police superin-tendent**

Contents

Acknowledgments

Rachel and I would like to express our deepest appreciation to the police leaders and agencies we have had the honor to work with and learn from over the years. Your relentless pursuit and dedication to improve the police profession is inspirational. We are grateful for the long-term relationships that we have developed with agencies around the country and look forward to continuing them along with creating new partnerships in the coming years.

Chapter One

Introduction

Crime reduction and community safety are important and noble responsibilities of the police. Police are confronted with the challenge of reducing crime and disorder while increasing community trust. It follows that what police do for crime reduction should be based on sound science and best practice. Research of police crime reduction efforts has proven that police can reduce crime.[1] However, addressing crime, disorder, quality-of-life issues, and community concerns in a systematic way that is sustained over time is a sophisticated process.

Implementing effective crime reduction requires deliberate thought and effort to integrate processes into the police organization, its culture, and the day-to-day work. The goal is to change a police organization from being reactive to proactive. However, police are in a tough position because their current long-established processes have been developed for answering calls and investigating crimes. Although these are two important and fundamental aspects of how the police serve the community, they are not enough, in themselves, to reduce crime.

The reality is that crime and disorder incidents cluster and concentrate into short-term and long-term problems that affect the community. Therefore, police are faced with addressing much more than just individual incidents and should take a broader perspective to be effective in crime reduction. To illustrate this point, Figure 1.1 is any typical jurisdiction showing the range of the individual incidents, short-term clusters, and long-term concentrations that occur.

Although this is only an example, it shows how crime and disorder incidents cluster and concentrate. All of these problems do exist and continually happen in every jurisdiction. The reason they happen in every community is because people and places are revictimized, and crimes are more likely to

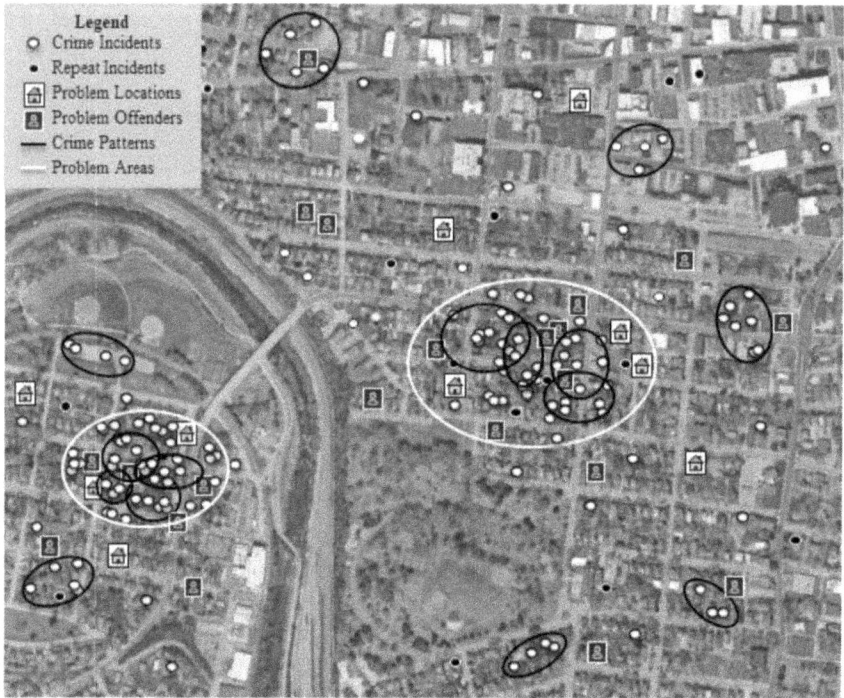

Figure 1.1. Clusters and Concentrations of Crime and Disorder.
Map. Google. (n.d.). Satellite Map. Retrieved February 7, 2020 from URL www.google.com/maps.

happen "near" other crimes in the short term.[2] In addition, crime concentrations occur in specific small areas, do not move around, and are persistent over time.[3] A contributing factor is that offenders repeatedly target people and places in areas near where they live and frequent most, and a small proportion of offenders account for a large proportion of crime.[4]

The map illustrates individual crime incidents throughout the jurisdiction, repeat incidents (i.e., repeat calls at the same address), crime patterns (i.e., short-term clusters of crime), and problem locations and areas (i.e., long-term concentrations of crime and disorder). The various symbols, as well as the small and large ellipses on the map, illustrate how these problems are pervasive across the jurisdiction and how in some areas they all continuously come together and overlapping over a long period of time.

In fact, crime and disorder problems will become larger if left alone when there is opportunity. Responses become more complex and difficult as the problems get larger. And, when problems are very large, they must be addressed at all levels simultaneously. Please forgive us as we use a fire analogy to make this point. The logic for addressing all of these problems is similar to how fires develop and are addressed.

When sparks of fire appear, they can be put out fairly easily. However, if they are not and there is fuel nearby, they can become small fires. Small fires require more effort to subdue, and when they are not addressed properly, they too can become larger fires. The larger the fire, the more difficult and complex the response is. A simple stomp with a shoe can put out a spark, and dirt can put out a small fire, but digging ditches and dropping chemicals from planes are often needed for the largest fires. Also, in very large and complicated fires, firefighters coordinate their responses and address all of these levels at the same time.

There are several relevant themes in this analogy that apply to crime reduction. That is, individual incidents of calls for service and crime are like sparks; short-term clusters of crime and disorder are like small fires; and long-term concentrations of crime and disorder are like larger fires. To be most effective, lower-level problems should be addressed so they do not get worse. Different and appropriate strategies based on the problem's complexity should be employed. Finally, an overall coordinated approach is needed to address all levels simultaneously with the goal to reduce crime and disorder in the entire jurisdiction.

The question is, are these problems being systematically identified and responded to properly? There is value in distinguishing short- and long-term problems for proactive crime reduction. By systematically identifying smaller, less complex problems and responding to them effectively, police can use resources more efficiently as crime and disorder incidents begin to cluster. The implementation of strategies derived from place-based, problem-solving, person-focused, and community-based approaches is what is needed to work. To be most effective, police have to implement all of these approaches collectively.[5]

But how do police bring evidence-based strategies together to address all of these problems and institutionalize them in the day-to-day operations of the police organization? Implementing just one approach can be challenging, so to incorporate multiple strategies and coordinate them within the police culture and structure is even more difficult. A significant barrier is that crime reduction is in direct competition with the ingrained culture of police responding to calls for service and investigating crimes.

Consequently, practical changes must be made across the entire organization to overcome certain aspects of police culture to institutionalize proactive crime reduction. If important, crime reduction must be purposefully incorporated along with the numerous responsibilities police have. It takes concerted effort because police must ensure that the organization operates in such a way that appropriate strategies are realistic and sustainable within and alongside other organizational practices.

Stratified Policing provides police a clear and concise solution to these challenges. This book is a culmination of our experiences as practitioners and researchers as well as our partnerships with many different police agencies across the United States to implement and institutionalize crime reduction. Stratified Policing[6] seeks to overcome these challenges and take advantage of the strengths of police practice. The primary goal is to institutionalize proactive crime reduction into police practice following a similar model police use for calls-for-service response.

Stratified Policing is an organizational model in which individuals operationalize problem-solving and evidence-based strategies in their day-to-day activities. As police do what is expected of them, proactive crime reduction becomes automatic. The model incorporates processes and strategies that have been proven to work and implements them realistically, efficiently, and effectively within the realities of police practice. As illustrated in Figure 1.2, it takes what we know works and "makes it work" in the police organization.

More specifically, Stratified Policing engages the entire police organization in the proactive process through a stratified approach. That is, specific tasks that individuals will do are based on rank and assignment. To illustrate the importance of how stratification brings together an organization to function as a cohesive team for crime reduction, we use an analogy to football.

Whether on the offensive or defensive side of the ball, each position has a role on the team, and each player has a specific job to do in each play. Specifi-

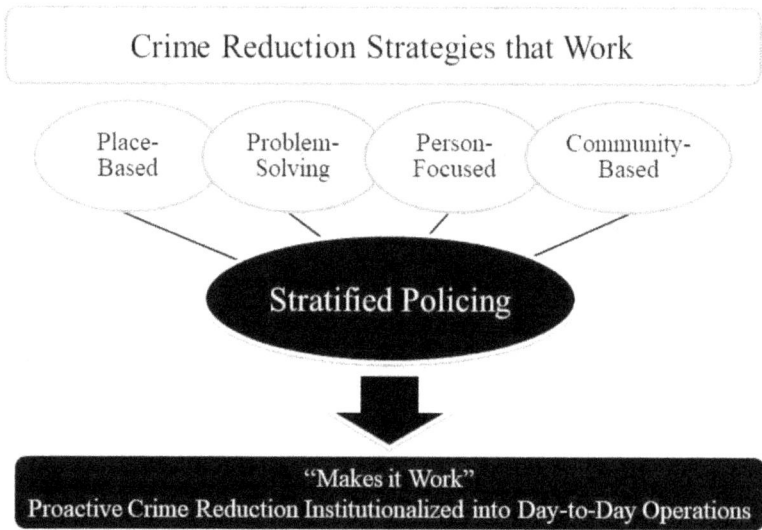

Figure 1.2. Stratified Policing and Proactive Crime Reduction.

cally, the offense's primary purpose is to move the ball down the field and to score a touchdown. The quarterback calls the plays and either hands off the ball to a running back, throws it to a receiver, or runs with it. Linemen protect the quarterback and block for the ball carriers. Running backs primarily run with the football, wide receivers elude defenders and catch the football, and tight ends are larger than wide receivers and either catch the football or block.

Depending on the position, the players are built physically different in order to accomplish their tasks well, but the tasks must be realistic and appropriate for both their position and abilities. For example, an NFL lineman who is 6'5" tall and 340 pounds would not be successful running down the field to catch a fifty-yard pass. Asking the lineman to even do this just once would not be reasonable based on his abilities and what he is already expected to do (i.e., block). This would only set the player up to fail. This task should be given to a wide receiver who is 6'1" tall, 185 pounds, and one of the quickest, elusive, and hand-skilled players on the field. So, in order for the team to be successful and win the game, players must do their jobs based on realistic expectations for their positions and abilities.

We see no difference in how a police organization should carry out proactive crime reduction. When individuals are asked to do tasks or be responsible for something that is unrealistic, they are essentially set up to fail. For example, it would not be fair or realistic to have an officer responsible to lead, coordinate resources, and work with community partners to address a long-term problem area. Instead, based on their positions and job responsibilities, police at every level should be asked to carry out proactive crime reduction realistically and implement responses that can be managed within their normal job duties and uncommitted time. This results in individuals from different ranks across the organization doing their specific jobs that build on one another. Together, this becomes a comprehensive approach to reduce crime.

Importantly, implementing a comprehensive system provides the means for police leaders to communicate a consistent, clear, and concise message of the rationale for change that helps to increase organizational commitment. Accountability is systematic and creates transparency with clear and realistic expectations. The two primary objectives of the accountability process are (1) to facilitate and ensure consistent and continual coordination of responses, and (2) to evaluate their appropriateness and effectiveness. This process creates an accountability loop that produces incentives at every level, so patrol officers, supervisors, managers, commanders, and executives all play their roles and do their jobs.

Stratified Policing changes the organizational culture and incorporates proactive crime reduction into everyday operations that are organized, systematic, and fair in the distribution of work and responsibility. Ultimately, an agency improves communication up, down, and across the organization, enhances transparency, and establishes clear accountability for carrying out proactive activities.[7] The following summarizes what Stratified Policing has been developed to accomplish:

1. Provide police leaders a clear path for implementation and institutionalization of proactive crime reduction modeled after current police processes.
2. Incorporate practical theory and evidence-based practices from place-based, problem-solving, person-focused, and community-based approaches.
3. Use crime analysis to identify and prioritize crime problems to be addressed realistically by different levels within the organization.
4. Lay out a specific and adaptable framework for incorporating small changes by rank and division into daily activities that all contribute to the larger practical approach.
5. Utilize time from individuals throughout the organization as a resource and become more efficient without requiring additional or specialized resources.
6. Ensure that individuals and divisions within the organization contribute based on what is realistic and neither is overburdened with responsibility or the work being done.
7. Incorporate multifaceted formal and informal accountability that is fair and transparent.
8. Raise the expectations for everyone in the organization to contribute to crime reduction.

In addition, Stratified Policing provides a framework that translates these ideas to institutionalize concrete concepts. They include the integration of evidence-based strategies as well as the stratification of crime and disorder problems, of crime analysis, of responsibility by rank, and of accountability. These concepts are translated even further into cohesive and consistent methods for approaching organizational change and implementing tangible processes and practices. The methods include developing agency crime reduction goals; systematic identification and analysis of problems; tailored evidence-based responses; assessment; and accountability meetings.

This book is written for police professionals. It incorporates theoretical concepts and results from rigorous research to provide the rationale, structure, and proactive strategies for what police can do to reduce crime. This sets the stage for explaining the model, framework, and methods of Stratified Policing, which is the result of our collective experience working both inside and alongside police agencies of different sizes, crime levels, and jurisdictions for many years. Roberto retired from a large police agency after twenty-two years and commanded various divisions—criminal investigations, patrol, special investigations, and professional standards. He is now an associate professor of criminal justice. Rachel was a crime analyst in a large department for several years and worked in Washington, DC, doing national-level research on crime analysis and policing. She is currently a professor of criminal justice.

The book contains nine additional chapters. Following this chapter, chapter 2 covers specific criminal justice theories that help police understand crime and criminals as well as the evidence-based proactive policing strategies that are derived from the theories. Chapter 3 is a discussion of our experience and observations about the challenges that some aspects of police culture pose to systematically implementing and sustaining proactive work. It ends with the rationale of why implementation of proactive crime reduction should mirror the current system of calls-for-service response in police organizations.

Chapter 4 provides both the model and framework of Stratified Policing. It defines important components and categories within them that make up the framework. Chapter 5 provides methods and specific parameters for developing and refining crime reduction goals of the agency. Chapters 6 through 9 follow a similar format and cover each level of problem and its processes for identification, analysis, response, assessment, and accountability. Chapter 6 presents immediate problems—significant incidents. Chapters 7 and 8 cover short-term problems—repeat incidents and crime patterns, respectively. Chapter 9 covers all long-term problems, which include problem offenders, problem locations, and problem areas. Finally, chapter 10 presents important organizational considerations for accountability and a detailed discussion of the overall accountability structure of meetings, their purposes, and evaluation measures.

NOTES

1. Weisburd, D., and Majmundar, M. K. (Eds.). (2018). *Proactive policing: Effects on crime and communities.* Washington, DC: The National Academies Press.

2. Johnson, S. D., and Bowers, K. J. (2004). The burglary as a clue to the future: The beginnings of prospective hot-spotting. *European Journal of Criminology, 1,* 237–55.

Johnson, S. D., Summers, L., and Pease, K. (2007). *Vehicle crime: Communicating spatial and temporal patterns.* London: Jill Dando Institute of Crime Science.

Johnson, S. D., Summers, L., and Pease, K. (2009). Offenders as forager: A direct test of the boost account of victimization. *Journal of Quantitative Criminology, 25,* 181–200.

Townsley, M., Homel, R., and Chaseling, J. (2003). Infectious burglaries: A test of the near repeat hypothesis. *British Journal of Criminology, 43,* 615–33.

3. Weisburd, D. (2015). The law of crime concentration and the criminology of place. *Criminology, 53*(2), 133–57.

4. Bernasco, W. (2008). Them again? Same-offender involvement in repeat and near repeat burglaries. *European Journal of Criminology, 5,* 411–31.

Bernasco, W. (2010). A sentimental journey to crime: Effects of residential history on crime location choice. *Criminology, 48*(2), 389–416.

Bernasco, W., and Nieuwbeerta, P. (2005). How do residential burglars select target areas? A new approach to the analysis of criminal location choice. *British Journal of Criminology, 44,* 296–315.

Johnson, S. D., and Summers, L. (2015). Testing ecological theories of offender spatial decision making using a discrete choice model. *Crime and Delinquency, 61*(3), 454–80.

5. Weisburd and Majmundar. *Proactive policing.*

6. Boba, R., and Santos, R. G. (2011). *A police organizational model for crime reduction: Institutionalizing problem solving, analysis, and accountability.* Washington, DC: US Department of Justice Office of Community-Oriented Policing Services.

7. Santos, R. G. (2018). Police organizational change after implementing crime analysis and evidence-based strategies through stratified policing. *Policing: A Journal of Policy and Practice, 12*(3), 288–302.

Chapter Two

Understanding Crime, Criminals, and What Works in Proactive Policing

Imagine going to a medical doctor for a health problem. In the conversation, the doctor says they have a "gut feeling" and recommends a surgical procedure that "should work." Now imagine going to another doctor who mentions that based on thirty years of research and medical practice, there is a particular surgical procedure that is evidence-based and will work. Which doctor to trust seems obvious when it is a decision about our health. But for some reason, such a choice is not so obvious when it comes to crime reduction. The police should take the same evidence-based approach when choosing strategies to reduce crime and make their communities safer. It is important for police to have knowledge about what works in preventing and reducing crime so that they can use approaches, strategies, and specific responses that are based on practical theories, systematic research, and effective police practice.

Thus, the purpose of this chapter is twofold. It provides the theoretical concepts and research that explain crime and offending. It also provides research results on the effectiveness of proactive policing approaches that are derived from these concepts. In doing so, it lays out the specific theories and strategies that are infused into Stratified Policing and serve as the foundation for its model, framework, and specific processes. This chapter helps police leaders explain why the agency is implementing proactive crime reduction strategies. It also helps those who are carrying out the strategies to understand how they are effective and worth doing.

UNDERSTANDING CRIME AND CRIMINALS

Most criminology theories are not relevant for police because they focus on why individuals become criminals based on a range of factors that are relatively abstract (i.e., lack of self-control, labeling, strain, learning, biological factors). Although these theories attempt to explain contributing factors underlying why some individuals choose to commit crimes, the reality is that it is both impractical and impossible for police to get to the heart of these causes and solve them. Police have no control over the background, family life, or other reasons that may explain why individuals have become offenders in the first place. Instead, they require theories that start with a motivated offender and explain how offenders make decisions to commit crime in the immediate situation. There are a few theories that have been supported by research that are directly related to effective crime reduction and have been translated to evidence-based police strategies.

Over the past forty years, significant developments have taken place through scholars' efforts to define and make sense of how crime events systematically happen in everyday life.[1] The resulting theories, together called "environmental criminology," contain important concepts that help explain why crimes systematically occur, how offenders' decisions to commit crime are made, and how offenders can be influenced not to commit crime.[2]

Environmental criminology focuses on the various aspects of the crime "environment" (i.e., the places and situations) in which crime occurs. Every city, town, and rural area can be divided into distinct places where particular behaviors are present and consistent over time. A key aspect of environmental criminology is that a crime can occur when an opportunity exists. For example, a theft cannot occur if there is nothing to steal; a battery cannot happen if there is no one to hit. It is within specific settings that routine behavior creates opportunities for crimes to occur in a systematic way. Some places contain more opportunities than others and contain more offenders who take advantage of opportunities.[3]

The goal of this group of theories is to help explain how opportunities come about as well as occur over time.[4] Their concepts are used by police to identify patterns of behavior in their jurisdictions. They also help understand how factors specific to the local environment create opportunities that lead to crime and other unwanted activity. With this understanding, police employ specific and effective strategies that are within their scope of influence to prevent these opportunities from arising as well as deter and apprehend offenders.

Problem Analysis Triangle

The foundation for understanding crime opportunities is structured around the problem analysis crime triangle.[5] The triangle explains problematic activity police are facing, either crime, disorder, or quality of life issues. Such events occur when a motivated offender and a victim (person) or target (type of property) come together at a particular place at a particular time. This triangle helps to explain the causes of immediate, short- and long-term problems where offenders take advantage of opportunities systematically.

The most important concept for police is that if a motivated offender, victim/target, and place are all needed for a crime to occur, removing one element can eliminate a crime from happening. Therefore, removing one element systematically can prevent multiple crimes in the long term. For example, even though there may be an offender and victim, if the police are present and in control of a place, a crime is less likely to happen. Equally important is understanding how the offender, victim/target, and place can be influenced within the crime setting and how opportunities can be prevented by individuals other than the police. The following are examples where one of the three elements needed for a crime is addressed:

> Police or security guards watch over people and property in semipublic places, such as stores or downtown areas. Individuals remove valuables from their cars. A bar owner with very strict policies does not allow underage drinking or over-serving to reduce drunk driving, fights, and sexual assaults. Police, parents, family members, parole officers, prosecutors, sports coaches, and clergy influence potential offenders' decisions to commit crime.

Although crime reduction strategies can include responses that influence all three components of the triangle, successfully impacting only one of the three can result in less crime. Settings for crime are often distinct and can be unique to a particular community, so the problem analysis triangle is an important tool that police use to deconstruct a problem to understand its causes. This helps them determine the most appropriate and effective strategies that they can employ themselves or with other criminal justice agencies and the community to resolve the problem. The triangle also ensures that police do not apply the same strategies to very different problems.

Rational Choice Theory

To understand offenders and their behavior in the immediate situation, we look to rational choice theory, which says offenders make choices about committing crimes based on anticipated risks and rewards.[6] The theory suggests, and research has found in most situations, that individuals will decide not to commit crimes when the risks are too high or the rewards are not adequate enough. Although different individuals will have varying levels of risk, each offender goes through the process of evaluating the risk of getting caught based on the immediate circumstances.

This theory is the basis of many crime prevention strategies. For example, asking citizens to remove valuables from their cars to reduce offenders' anticipated rewards. One of the most often used by police is directed patrol, which can influence offenders' perceptions of risk that being caught is too high for the anticipated reward. Understanding why individuals choose or don't choose to commit crimes in specific situations is important for developing strategies that influence their decision-making process.

Crime Pattern Theory

Crime pattern theory helps explain how criminal events will most likely occur in or around areas where offenders routinely spend their time (e.g., where they live).[7] The theory asserts that offenders commit crimes in places they know and explains why multiple crimes cluster in small areas. The theory shows that criminal events will most likely occur in areas where the activity space of potential offenders overlaps with the activity space of potential victims/targets. An individual's activity space is that area that becomes familiar through everyday activities. There are a range of studies in different jurisdictions that consistently support this theory and find that offenders are more likely to commit crimes in areas they currently live.[8]

Crime pattern theory taps into human nature and our tendencies to develop a routine and pattern of behavior in small geographic areas. For example, most people go to bed, wake up, and go about their business at a particular time, shop at the same grocery store, and meet friends at the same places. Usually, they choose what is acceptable and most convenient, which typically is close to where they live. Offenders do the same thing for their everyday routine activities. However, as offenders go about their day, they take advantage of opportunities to commit crime in their activity space. This is why when there is a concentration of chronic repeat offenders living in a relatively small area, there will be a concentration of crime.[9] The practical implications of this idea are that the police should look for offenders who live where crime clusters occur and/or frequent places during their routine activities.

Law of Crime Concentration

In addition to what the research finds about offenders, research to test these theories also provides consistent findings about how crime happens at places. The "law of crime concentration" is a conclusion based on more than thirty years of research which states, "for a defined measure of crime at a specific micro-geographic unit, the concentration of crime will fall within a narrow bandwidth of percentages for a defined cumulative proportion of crime."[10] This is an academic way of saying not only do we know crime does cluster by place, but the concentrations are specific small areas, that do not move around, and persist over time. Thus, while understanding offenders, their routine activities, and their decisions to commit crime in the immediate situation is important, the law of crime concentration confirms it is also worthwhile for police to focus on places in order to reduce crime.

Repeat Victimization, Near Repeats, and the 80/20 Rule

If opportunities for crime are created by routine behavior, then victimization is as well. Repeat victimization refers to the recurrence of crime in the same places or against the same people.[11] Research shows both people and places previously victimized are more likely to be victimized again than those that have never been victimized.[12] The best predictor for victimization is that the person or place has been victimized before.[13] Thus, victimization is an important indicator of future victimization, and the practical implications for police are that repeat victimization of people and places is a worthy focus of proactive crime reduction efforts.

Even further, research has established that not only are places revictimized individually, but crimes are more likely to happen "near" other crimes in the short term.[14] Most near repeat research focuses on property crime (e.g., residential burglary and theft from vehicle), and there are consistent findings with important implications for police. Houses on the same block as a burgled home are at a substantially higher risk of being burglarized. This is often caused by offenders returning to the area of a prior successful burglary and choosing targets that are most convenient to them near places they have already hit. These findings imply that police should proactively identify clusters of near repeats, because crimes are likely to continue and be committed by the same offenders.[15]

The 80/20 rule is another important concept. It means generally that 80 percent of outcomes are the result of only 20 percent of the related causes. This occurs often in nature; for example, a small proportion of the earthquakes are responsible for a very large proportion of the world's earthquake-related damage. Research consistently finds the 80/20 rule applies to crime. A small number of locations accounts for a large number of crime events; and a small proportion of offenders accounts for a large proportion of offenses.[16] These findings and application of the 80/20 rule direct police to focus on a small proportion of areas, places/victims, and offenders where crime is concentrated to get the most out of their crime reduction efforts.

Spatial Displacement and Diffusion of Benefits

When police introduce strategies where crime concentrates, there is often the misconception that those who are committing crimes will just move to another area and commit the same amount of crime. This is referred to as spatial displacement of crime, and the possibility of this occurring is usually a concern for police. Extensive research has been done to test spatial displacement in areas with short-term clusters and long-term concentrations of crime. The findings consistently show when strategies are implemented by police in specific areas, they do not result in statistically significant displacement of crime.[17] For the sake of simplifying these research results, let's just say an offender commits a set number of crimes a month in an area. An effective police response in this area will result in three outcomes: (1) the offender commits no more crimes, (2) the offender stays in the area and commits fewer crimes, or (3) the offender leaves the area and commits even fewer crimes. Any of these three outcomes results in less crime without moving the same amount of crime to a different area.

Research also confirms what often occurs instead of displacement is a diffusion of benefits.[18] That is, when the opportunities for crime are reduced in a particular area, there is a positive impact on crime that extends beyond the area where the response is actually implemented. Consequently, the implications for police are that when they implement strategies in short-term clusters or long-term, high-crime areas, crime can be reduced, and there will likely be a positive impact on nearby areas.

WHAT WORKS IN PROACTIVE CRIME REDUCTION

In 2017, the National Academy of Sciences brought researchers and police experts together to review all known research and consider best practices to make conclusions about what is effective in proactive crime reduction. The comprehensive report entitled *Proactive Policing: Effects on Crime and Communities* organizes and summarizes what is known about "what works" to date.[19] The report defines proactive policing as "all policing strategies that have as one of their goals the prevention or reduction of crime and disorder and that are not reactive in terms of focusing primarily on uncovering ongoing crime or on investigating or responding to crimes once they have occurred."[20] Proactive strategies are those that emphasize prevention, are implemented based on police initiative, and focus on the underlying factors that may be contributing to crime and disorder.

The report breaks proactive policing into four categories: place-based, problem-solving, person-focused, and community-based strategies. Throughout the Stratified Policing framework, these strategies are incorporated where they have been found to be most effective. We provide an overview of these proactive policing strategies as the evidence-based foundation for Stratified Policing. These strategies are discussed in future chapters where they are operationalized into the police organization through the framework and its processes. The purpose here is to provide a description of each approach, along with research results.

Place-Based Approach

The place-based approach is an outgrowth of theory and research that establishes that crime concentrates by place in both the short and the long term. The predominant place-based strategy employed by police is "hot spots policing." Its primary objective is to prevent and deter crime in small areas. The strategy is implemented by identifying specific areas that have disproportionately more crime than other areas within a jurisdiction over the long term and focus police responses in those areas.[21]

Long-term hot spots that are typically identified are relatively small areas, such as individual locations, groups of streets, as well as areas within neighborhoods and commercial corridors. Responses range from primarily police resources, such as directed patrol, field contacts, and proactive arrests, to long-term responses that are implemented through partnerships with the community.[22] Another way the approach is implemented is by identifying micro-time hot spots (i.e., short-term), which differ from long-term hot spots. These micro-time hot spots are defined by the emergence of several closely related crime incidents within a few minutes' travel distance from one another that occur within one to two weeks, in other words, a crime "flare-up."[23] Responses to micro-time hot spots can be similar to those for long-term hot spots.[24]

The goal of policing in both short- and long-term hot spots is to focus limited resources on the hardest hit crime areas in order to have the most impact and the best return on a police department's investment in resources. Overwhelmingly, the research shows hot spots policing is effective in reducing crime. There is extensive research on long-term hot spots that includes experimental, quasi-experimental, and evaluation studies. They consistently show proactive responses reduce crime in these areas, do not have negative effects on the citizens who live in the hot spots, and do not displace the crime to other areas.[25] Research on response in micro-time hot spots is not as plentiful, but is strong. Results from experimental and quasi-experimental studies show crime is reduced with no spatial displacement and crime reduction remains after the responses are stopped.[26]

Problem-Solving Approach

The problem-solving approach addresses specific long-term crime, disorder, and quality-of-life problems. It uses the problem analysis triangle to understand opportunities that give rise to each problem. Responses are specifically tailored based on the analysis, and the objective is to prevent crime by deterring and reducing opportunities.[27] The police use a specific process, called SARA, in this approach.

SARA includes four steps: (S)canning and defining specific problems, (A)nalyzing data to understand the underlying routine behavior that creates the problem, (R)esponding to the problem using both police and nonpolice methods, and (A)ssessing whether the response has worked.[28] Formal crime analysis is used to identify, analyze, and assess the impact on crime and disorder. Developed from the environmental criminology theories, situational crime prevention responses[29] are implemented often in collaboration with external partners. That is, responses address underlying causes of the problem. In most cases, traditional police activities, such as directed patrol and arrest, are supplemented with more in-depth responses that engage citizens, business owners, community groups, and other nonpolice entities. Problems are defined very specifically, so responses can be focused.

Research on the effectiveness of the problem-solving approach is based mostly on practical evaluations of police problem-solving efforts for a wide range of problems.[30] The research suggests the approach has strong effects on crime. Researchers and police experts agree that regardless of the type of problem addressed the SARA process is valuable.[31] There is also important work that has been done over the last twenty years bringing together the research and best practices in the form of guidebooks for common problems that police face. Each guidebook breaks down a specific problem using the problem analysis triangle, provides a list of responses that have been successful, and outlines ways to analyze and adapt the responses to the local environment.[32]

Person-Focused Approach

The person-focused approach is based on the 80/20 rule and research showing crime concentrates by offenders. It is centered on the idea that a small number of offenders commit a large proportion of the crime.[33] The primary objective for person-focused crime reduction is to prevent crime by deterring specific and known high-rate offenders.[34] Strategies implemented by police include repeat offender programs and what is called "focus deterrence."[35] A problem-solving approach is used so that high-crime offenders are identified. Police tailor responses for each offender based on who they are and their circumstances in order to deter them from committing future crimes.

The central responses by police include "direct interaction with offenders and communication of clear incentives for compliance and consequences for criminal activity."[36] Police often confront offenders to explicitly outline what will happen if they continue committing crime. Organized face-to-face meetings with offenders are conducted along with family, community members, and others to reinforce the seriousness of the process and compliance.[37] Other responses include contacting offenders at their homes, on the street, or in jail.[38] While many of the deterrence strategies target gangs and groups of drug offenders, they have also been implemented for property crime offenders.[39] Research suggests focused deterrence programs do result in short- and long-term reductions in crime, particularly for gang violence and street crime related to drug markets.[40] It also shows individual repeat offending is reduced.

Community-Based Approach

In the community-based approach, police engage the community to identify and control crime.[41] "Community-oriented policing" is the most commonly known community-based strategy. It is a philosophy that promotes organizational strategies that support the systematic use of partnerships and problem-solving techniques, to proactively address the immediate conditions that can escalate into public safety issues such as crime, disorder, and fear of crime.[42] The key components are developing relationships and partnerships with the community to understand and respond to problems as well as to engender collaboration and increase legitimacy of and trust in the police.[43]

There is a wide range of programs and responses that are associated with the community-based approach, such as DARE, neighborhood watch, coffee with a cop, national night out, and shop with a cop. Other responses focus on increasing the flow of information to and from citizens through community meetings, officers walking the "beat," talking to residents, and providing crime and safety information to the public through social media.[44] In essence, community-based approaches seek to improve police transparency and the quality of everyday interactions between the police and the community to increase collaboration and trust.

The evidence suggests when community involvement is coupled with problem-solving approaches it can be effective.[45] More importantly, researchers conclude these strategies have positive effects on the satisfaction of citizens with the police and their trust in the police (i.e., increases police legitimacy).[46] This conclusion makes the community-based approach essential. In order for police to employ proactive crime reduction effectively, the community must trust what they are doing. The police responses should be seen as positive and their authority as legitimate. Simply put, the more effective community-based strategies are, the easier it will be to systematically implement place-based, person-focused, and problem-solving approaches.

Crime Analysis

Crime analysis is the process of examining data and making conclusions that guide proactive crime reduction strategies; however, it is not a strategy by itself. Similar to how a radiologist examines MRI results and passes them to the doctor treating a patient, crime analysts examine crime data and pass results to police who implement proactive strategies. Crime analysis has a significant role in proactive crime reduction because, as the evidence shows, for police strategies to be effective, they must be focused in a systematic way through the crime analysis process.[47]

Even further, to support these approaches, crime analysis should either direct a specific evidence-based response (i.e., action-oriented), or indicate whether responses are working (i.e., evaluation-oriented) Crime analysis results should be obvious in their purpose simply based on their content. When crime analysis for crime reduction is action-oriented, it evokes a specific evidence-based response (i.e., directed patrol in a specific area). On the other hand, evaluation-oriented crime analysis includes meaningful measures and straightforward statistics that are specific to the problem and response being evaluated.

Crime Reduction Accountability

CompStat was developed by the NYPD with the goal to create a formal accountability structure to hold precinct commanders accountable for reducing crime occurring in their areas.[48] It is widely accepted as one of the most important policing innovations in the last century.[49] Now, more than twenty-five years after NYPD introduced CompStat, the need to have an internal process to hold police accountable for reducing crime is accepted by police agencies around the United States and internationally. Over the years, many agencies have adopted variations of CompStat to fit their needs, such as employing a more collaborative process and not solely relying on crime counts to assess effectiveness (e.g., week-to-week, current week to the same week last year).

Yet, the best way to implement accountability into individual agencies based on their unique characteristics and community is still elusive. Many agencies hold some type of meeting where crime statistics and crime reduction responses are discussed. The goal is to enforce accountability and to evaluate the effectiveness of the strategies implemented. However, the research on the implementation of accountability models for crime reduction indicates there is a lack of direction in that there are often not clear expectations or guidance for district commanders on how to accomplish their goals.[50] Another concern is the approaches do not involve lower-ranking personnel, but place heavy emphasis on commanders. Lower ranks do not have clear roles, are not engaged in the process, and may not know what is expected of them.[51]

Over the years, we have seen agencies implement accountability approaches a range of different ways as well as start, stop, revamp, and start them again, or just quit them altogether. Our general observation is that police understand that accountability is important, but they struggle with trying to balance a collaborative versus punitive approach as well as realistic expectations with the pressure to achieve them. We believe that to be meaningful and effective, an accountability process needs to overcome these issues. The process should include transparency, collaboration, clear and realistic evaluation, and well-defined methods to achieve success that incorporate all ranks in the organization. While an accountability process does not by itself reduce crime, it is clear that it is an essential component that ensures proactive crime reduction work gets done, is efficient, and is effective.

CONCLUSION

There is more than enough evidence to support police adopting proactive strategies to reduce crime. When police focus on high-crime areas, high-rate offenders, and large problems in their communities, there is consistent evidence that they are effective. When police incorporate community-based strategies as well, they are effective in improving trust between the police and the community and increasing police legitimacy.[52]

Importantly, to be the most effective, police should employ a combination of approaches based on what they are trying to do and what types of problems they are facing. But how do police bring all of these theories, research results, and evidence-based practices together and implement them in the police organization? That is, implementing just one of these approaches can be challenging, so to incorporate multiple strategies and coordinate them within the police culture and structure is even more difficult. Consequently, Stratified Policing is an organizational solution that incorporates crime analysis and an accountability structure to institutionalize processes for implementing proactive place-based, problem-solving, person-focused, and community-based strategies into everyday police practice.

NOTES

1. Felson, M., and Boba, R. (2010). *Crime and everyday life.* Thousand Oaks, CA: Sage.

2. Brantingham, P. J., and Brantingham, P. L. (1982). *Environmental criminology.* Thousand Oaks, CA: Sage

3. Cohen, L., and Felson, M. (1979). Social change and crime rate trends: A routine activity approach. *American Sociological Review, 44*(4), 588–608.

4. Felson and Boba. *Crime and everyday life.*

5. Center for Problem-Oriented Policing (2020), Retrieved on July 31, 2020 from www.popcenter.asu.edu/.

6. Felson, M., and Clarke, R. V. (1998). *Opportunity makes the thief: Practical theory for crime prevention* (Police Research Series Paper 98). London: Home Office, Research, Development and Statistics Directorate, Policing and Reducing Crime Unit.

7. Brantingham, P. L., and Brantingham, P. J. (1990). Situational crime prevention in practice. *Canadian Journal of Criminology, 32,* 17–40.

8. Bernasco, W. (2008). Them again? Same-offender involvement in repeat and near repeat burglaries. *European Journal of Criminology, 5,* 411–31.

Bernasco, W. (2010). A sentimental journey to crime: Effects of residential history on crime location choice. *Criminology, 48*(2), 389–416.

Bernasco, W., and Nieuwbeerta, P. (2005). How do residential burglars select target areas? A new approach to the analysis of criminal location choice. *British Journal of Criminology, 44,* 296–315.

Johnson, S. D., and Summers, L. (2015). Testing ecological theories of offender spatial decision making using a discrete choice model. *Crime and Delinquency, 61*(3), 454–80.

9. Johnson, S. D., Summers, L., and Pease, K. (2009). Offenders as forager: A direct test of the boost account of victimization. *Journal of Quantitative Criminology, 25,* 181–200.

10. Weisburd, D. (2015). The law of crime concentration and the criminology of place. *Criminology, 53*(2), 133–57.

11. Farrell, G., and Pease, K. (1993). *Once bitten, twice bitten: Repeat victimization and its implications for crime prevention* (Crime Prevention Unit Series Paper 46). London: Home Office, Police Research Group.

12. Grove, L. E., Farrell, G., Farrington, D. P., and Johnson, S. D. (2012). *Preventing repeat victimisation: A systematic review.* Stockholm: Bra—The Swedish National Council for Crime Prevention.

13. Johnson, S. D., Guerette, R. T., and Bowers, K. (2014). Crime displacement: What we know, what we don't know, and what it means for crime reduction. *Journal of Experimental Criminology, 10*(4), 549–71.

14. Johnson, S. D., and Bowers, K. J. (2004). The burglary as a clue to the future: The beginnings of prospective hot-spotting. *European Journal of Criminology, 1,* 237–55.

Johnson, S. D., Summers, L., and Pease, K. (2007). *Vehicle crime: Communicating spatial and temporal patterns*. London: Jill Dando Institute of Crime Science.

Johnson, Summers, and Pease Offenders as forager.

Townsley, M., Homel, R., and Chaseling, J. (2003). Infectious burglaries: A test of the near repeat hypothesis. *British Journal of Criminology, 43*, 615–33.

15. Chainey, S. P., Curtis-Ham, S. J., Evans, R. M., and Burns, G. J. (2018). Examining the extent to which repeat and near repeat patterns can prevent crime. *Policing: An International Journal, 41*(5), 608–22.

Coupe, T., and Blake, L. (2006). Daylight and darkness targeting strategies and the risks of being seen at residential burglaries. *Criminology, 44*, 431–64.

Johnson, S. D., Lab, S., and Bowers, K. J. (2008). Stable and fluid hot spots of crime: Differentiation and identification. *Built Environment, 34*(1), 32–46.

16. Clarke, R. V., and Eck, J. (2005). *Crime analysis for problem solvers: In 60 small steps.* Washington, DC: US Department of Justice Office of Community-Oriented Policing Services.

17. Johnson, Guerette, and Bowers. Crime displacement, 549–71.

Santos, R. G., and Santos, R. B. (2015). An ex post facto evaluation of tactical police response in residential theft from vehicle micro-time hot spots. *Journal of Quantitative Criminology, 31*(4), 679–98.

Santos, R. G., and Santos, R. B. (2015). Practice-based research: Ex post facto evaluation of evidence-based police practices implemented in residential burglary micro-time hot spots. *Evaluation Review, 39*(5), 451–79.

Santos, R. B., and Santos, R. G. (2020). Proactive police response in property crime micro-time hot spots: Results from a partially-blocked blind random control trial. *Journal of Quantitative Criminology*, 1–21. DOI 10.1007/s10940-020-09456-8.

18. Clarke, R. V., and Weisburd, D. (1994). Diffusion of crime control benefits: Observations on the reverse of displacement. In R. V. Clarke. (Ed.) *Crime prevention studies* (vol. 2, pp. 165–83). Monsey, NY: Criminal Justice Press.

19. Weisburd, D., and Majmundar, M. K. (Eds.) (2018). *Proactive policing: Effects on crime and communities.* Washington, DC: The National Academies Press.

20. Weisburd and Majmundar. *Proactive policing,* 30.

21. Braga, A. A., Turchan, B., Papachristos, A. V., and Hureau, D. M. (2019). Hot spots policing of small geographic areas effects on crime. *Campbell Systematic Reviews.* DOI: 10.1002/cl2.1046.

22. Braga, Turchan, Papachristos, and Hureau. Hot spots policing.

23. Santos and Santos. An ex post facto evaluation of tactical police response.

24. Santos, R. B., and Santos, R. G. (2015). Examination of police dosage in residential burglary and theft from vehicle micro-time hot spots. *Crime Science, 4*(27), 1–12.

Santos and Santos. Practice-based research: Ex post facto evaluation.

Santos and Santos. An ex post facto evaluation of tactical police response.

25. Weisburd and Majmundar. *Proactive policing.*

26. Santos and Santos. Examination of police dosage in residential burglary.

Santos and Santos. Practice-based research: Ex post facto evaluation.

Santos and Santos. An ex post facto evaluation of tactical police response.

Santos and Santos. Proactive police response.

27. Goldstein, H. (1990). *Problem-oriented policing.* New York: McGraw-Hill. Weisburd and Majmundar. *Proactive policing.*

28. Eck, J., and Spelman, W. (1987). *Problem solving: Problem-oriented policing in Newport News.* Washington, DC: Police Executive Research Forum.

Center for Problem-Oriented Policing. https://popcenter.asu.edu/.

29. Clarke, R. V. (1980). Situational crime prevention: Theory and practice. *British Journal of Criminology, 20,* 136–47.

Clarke, R. V. (Ed.) (1997). *Situational crime prevention: Successful case studies.* New York: Harrow and Heston.

30. Weisburd and Majmundar. *Proactive policing.*

Weisburd, D., Telep, C. W., Hinkle, J. C., and Eck, J. (2010). Is problem-oriented policing effective in reducing crime and disorder? Findings from a Campbell systematic review. *Criminology and Public Policy, 9*(1), 139–72.

31. Weisburd and Majmundar. *Proactive policing.*

Scott, M. (2010). Evaluating the effectiveness of problem-oriented policing. *Criminology and Public Policy, 9*(1), 135–37.

32. See Arizona State University's Center for Problem-Oriented Policing (https://popcenter.asu.edu/) and the Office of Community-Oriented Policing Resource Center (https://cops.usdoj.gov/ric/ric.php) for copies of these guidebooks.

33. Braga, A., and Weisburd, D. (2012). The effects of focused deterrence strategies on crime: A systematic review and meta-analysis of the empirical evidence. *Journal of Research in Crime and Delinquency, 49*(3), 323–58.

34. Weisburd and Majmundar. *Proactive policing.*

35. Braga and Weisburd. The effects of focused deterrence strategies on crime.

36. Weisburd and Majmundar. *Proactive policing*, 58.

37. Wallace, D., Papachristos, A. V., Meares, T., and Fagan, J. (2016). Desistance and legitimacy: The impact of offender notification meetings on recidivism among high risk offenders. *Justice Quarterly, 33*(7), 1237–64.

38. Groff, E. R., Ratcliffe, J. H., Haberman, C. P., Sorg, E. T., Joyce, N. M., and Taylor, R. B. (2015). Does what police do at hot spots matter? The Philadelphia policing tactics experiment. *Criminology, 53*(1), 23–53.

39. Santos, R. B., and Santos, R. G. (2016). Offender-focused police strategies in residential burglary and theft from vehicle hot spots: A partially blocked randomized controlled trial. *Journal of Experimental Criminology, 12*(3), 373–402.

40. Weisburd and Majmundar. *Proactive policing.*

41. Weisburd and Majmundar. *Proactive policing.*

42. Cordner, G. W. (2014). Community policing. In M. Reisig and R. Kane. (Eds.) *The Oxford handbook of police and policing* (pp. 148–71). New York: Oxford University Press.

43. Santos, R. G. (2019). *Community-oriented policing for police supervisors.* Washington, DC: Department of Justice, Office of Community-Oriented Policing Services.

44. Skogan, W. G. (2019). Advocate: Community policing. In D. L. Weisburd and A. A. Braga. (Eds.) *Police innovation: Contrasting perspectives* (pp. 27–44). New York: Cambridge University Press.

45. Weisburd and Majmundar. *Proactive policing.*

46. Gill, Weisburd, Telep, Vitter, and Bennett. Community-oriented policing to reduce crime.

47. Santos, R. B. (2014). The effectiveness of crime analysis for crime reduction: Cure or diagnosis? *Journal of Contemporary Criminal Justice, 30*(2), 147–68.

48. Weisburd, D., Mastrofski, S. D., McNally, A. M., Greenspan, R., and Willis, J. J. (2003). Reforming to preserve: Compstat and strategic problem solving in American policing. *Criminology and Public Policy, 2,* 421–56.

49. Shah, S., Burch, J., and Neusteter, S. R. (2018). *Leveraging CompStat to include community measures in police performance management. Perspectives from the field.* New York: Vera Institute of Justice.

50. Shah, Burch, and Neusteter. *Leveraging CompStat.*

51. Dabney, D. (2010). Observations regarding key operational realities in a Compstat model of policing. *Justice Quarterly, 27,* 28–51.

Willis, J. J., Mastrofski, S. D., and Kochel, T. R. (2010). The co-implementation of CompStat and community policing. *Journal of Criminal Justice, 38,* 969–80.

52. Weisburd and Majmundar. *Proactive policing,* 12.

Chapter Three

Police Culture
and Proactive Crime Reduction

There are some common challenges that police agencies face when implementing evidence-based proactive crime reduction strategies. Even when a strategy has been found to work, that does not mean it will be easily or effectively implemented. It is not as easy as it may seem to translate important concepts and practices of effective strategies to real-life police work. This is because it can be tougher than anticipated to bring in new ideas, change practices, and sustain them to make an entire agency proactive. Some of the difficulties of institutionalizing crime reduction throughout an organization lie in the culture of policing and are the same ones that make other types of changes difficult as well.

In this chapter, we talk about how some aspects of police culture can be barriers to institutionalizing proactive crime reduction. This sets the stage for the next chapter when we talk about how Stratified Policing has been created in an attempt to overcome these barriers and take advantage of the strengths of police practice. In order to make police organizations proactive, police leaders must understand the challenges and look to the current processes that work in policing so they can be adapted and applied in the agency appropriately and realistically for crime reduction.

CULTURAL BARRIERS TO INSTITUTIONALIZING
PROACTIVE CRIME REDUCTION

As discussed in chapter 2, police and research experts assert that to be effective in crime reduction, police agencies cannot simply prescribe one approach. Instead, police should implement the place-based, problem-based, person-focused, and community-based approaches together and tailor them to the needs of the community.[1] Incorporating the elements necessary to institutionalize crime reduction strategies can be a difficult process. There are no conventional practices or clear direction from research or police practice about how to implement this combination of approaches. Police leaders cannot assume that symbolically committing to a proactive approach, such as hot spots policing or focused deterrence, will result in the rank and file incorporating new strategies into their day-to-day operations. Leaders must make practical decisions based on the structure, current operations, and resources of their agencies to overcome ingrained aspects of police culture that can be barriers to institutionalization and organizational change.

Systematic Crime Reduction Cannot Be Implemented Easily

For some reason, when it comes to proactive crime reduction it is often assumed once police leaders articulate that a new approach is being implemented in the organization, the idea will become part of everyone's day-to-day practice. In many cases, police leaders make the mistake of underestimating what is needed to introduce and institutionalize new evidence-based initiatives. Oftentimes, there an assumption that changes in organizational culture are not necessary to normalize crime reduction efforts. Yet, not making changes to influence day-to-day behavior is a missed opportunity. Often, if these changes are not made, over time, a new crime reduction initiative will fail and never become part of the daily routine.

To compensate for the need to make organizational changes, police leaders often create a specialized unit by handpicking a motivated supervisor(s) and a group of high-performing officers to conduct crime reduction. The unit then serves as the predominant proactive arm of the organization, and the approach is considered "implemented." This can be problematic in a few ways. What often happens is that these units morph into some type of "tact" unit with no clear direction. They slowly divert from their purpose as well as get pulled in different directions by commanders, work hours and days that best fit the unit, and do not accomplish their original mission. Even in the best case scenario, pulling already limited resources from other areas and creating a unit to serve as the proactive arm of the agency is just not enough to be successful in long-term systematic crime reduction.

Another negative result from creating a specialized unit is that it sends the message to the rest of the organization that no one but the specialized unit is responsible for proactive crime reduction. Obviously, this is not the way to implement an organization-wide approach and create true organizational change. With that said, it is understandable why it may seem appealing to create a specialized unit since it is very easy to do so. This is in stark contrast to changing the organization's culture where everyone has a specific job and role to play in an overall organizational model. When an organization becomes proactive, specialized units serve in a supportive role and play their small part in the entire process.

Another common compensation for organizational change is that some police leaders purchase software and rely on the technology in an attempt to quickly make their organizations become proactive. An example of this is crime-mapping dashboard software. The goal of purchasing this software is that once everyone has access to crime data, they will analyze it themselves and respond proactively. Unfortunately, in reality this is often not the case. Software and/or technology, by itself, will not change the culture of the organization. At best, it will be extremely underutilized. At worst, it can be counterproductive to the process of institutionalizing crime reduction. There is no way around it that substantive changes across the entire organization are needed in order to institutionalize crime reduction. Therefore, a comprehensive approach with a framework and specific methods is required for the best chance of success in changing an organization's established culture to one that infuses multiple evidence-based strategies simultaneously.

Crime Reduction Activities Have Stiff Competition

There are so many things that police deal with that can draw focus and resources away from systematically conducting proactive crime reduction. It does not take long to see how proactive work can be surpassed by what police are expected to do day to day. There are many examples of calls for service, many of which are not law enforcement related, follow-up investigations, and administrative duties that police at all levels are tasked to do and expected to assist with but are not related to proactive crime reduction. When we look at most police agencies from a "30,000 foot view," a very small amount of time is allocated to conducting proactive work.

We argue if crime reduction is important, it must be deliberately integrated along with the innumerable other responsibilities of police. There are many things that are easily prioritized over crime reduction because they are already integrated into what police do. Many of these are not directly related to proactive crime reduction and, in fact, can pull resources away from proactive work. Therefore, it takes concerted effort for police to implement and sustain a crime reduction approach. This effort must ensure that police organizations operate in such a way that appropriate strategies are realistic and sustainable within the organizational practices. With all of this in mind, we think it is safe to say that doing proactive crime reduction has stiff competition.

Organizational Change Can Be Difficult in Police Organizations

A strong argument can be made that organizational change within a police agency is much more difficult than in a private company. Two key reasons stand out. The first is that policing is not driven by profit. The second is that changes have to be accomplished with the existing workforce because there is very little opportunity to add, remove, or replace people who are resistant and/or unwilling to adapt to change. In contrast, private businesses, in one way or another, are driven and sustained by their profits year to year. For these businesses, there are real consequences for not being able to create, change, and adapt.

It is also easier for private companies to convince employees why change must occur. Since people's livelihoods depend on success and profits made by the company, there is more individual motivation to comply and do what is necessary day to day. In these circumstances, the ability of individuals being to adjust and actively assist in change is vitally important to the individuals themselves. Since there are direct negative outcomes for not adjusting to the change, individuals are much more motivated to adapt in a private versus a public organization.

Even further, it is easier for private sector leaders to move, demote, remove, and replace employees based on performance and/or their inability to adapt. However, with very few exceptions, police executives do not have this type of flexibility when they try to make systematic organizational change. They must incorporate changes with the workforce they already have. The amount of personnel and individuals in certain ranks tends to remain the same, and executives have very little freedom to make substantive changes to either.

In many cases, even if certain changes could improve the organization, playing it safe or not taking too many risks by sticking to current culture and practice is more favorable. The likelihood of a police organization going out of business because of a failure to reduce crime is virtually nonexistent. These are important cultural factors because they can give the impression that there are no consequences for people's lack of innovation, inability to change, or apathy toward the change process.

It cannot be taken lightly that any innovative strategy will be in direct competition with the ingrained culture of police responding to calls for service, investigating crimes, and making arrests. This direct competition creates conflict and resistance that prevents institutionalizing new, better, and effective crime reduction practices. This resistance can occur due to individual uncertainty about the change process and how the change affects them personally. When attempting organizational change, police leaders need to take an organizational approach that provides specific processes to enforce/re-enforce a structure that encourages and expects certain behaviors. This must be applied equally across the workforce and be realistic in the context of the other work being done. The good news is that a strength of the police culture is that police officers at every rank work very well in a strongly structured environment with specific rules and policies—and the more specific, the better.

Thus, in the police organization, it is essential to have clear rules and expectations of work that needs to be done, well-defined processes, and established measures of success to reduce the conflict and resistance that can be generated from uncertainty. It improves the likelihood that individuals will cooperate and make the changes asked of them. We cannot stress enough the importance of transparency and role clarity in police processes. The success of organizational change will rely heavily on individuals' abilities to understand their roles and responsibilities in the context of proactive crime reduction.

Consequently, implementing a framework provides the means for police leaders to communicate a consistent, clear, and concise message of the rationale for change that helps to increase organizational commitment. A concise framework provides focus to the message so that change is observable in day-to-day operations through defined roles and set expectations for each individual. Organizational change is difficult, and there is no room for vagueness or lack of direction when engaging individuals in the process. But when successful, an organizational framework that changes people's behavior will in time change their thinking as well.

Line-Level Officers Doing All of the Crime Reduction Work Is Unrealistic

This is how proactive crime reduction implementation often looks: Chief says, "Captain, reduce crime." Captain says, "Lieutenant, we need to reduce crime." Lieutenant says, "Sergeant, we need to reduce crime." Sergeant says, "Officer, I am not sure what they want us to do, but we need to reduce crime." Officer thinks, "How am I supposed to reduce crime in between calls, police reports, arrests, backups, and court?"

In many cases, this is not that far from reality. Unfortunately, the mistake of pushing the responsibility to the line-level officer is common and, we would argue, practically impossible to implement successfully and sustainably. It is not only impractical, but also is unfair and unreasonable to expect officers to be solely responsible for reducing crime throughout a community. There are two key reasons why this is not effective. First, line-level officers are already responsible for a large proportion of what police already do for the community—answering calls for service, investigating crimes, providing services (e.g., holiday house checks, funeral services, etc.), responding to critical incidents, natural disasters, and so on. Their workdays are filled with activities in the field or in the criminal justice system, and their tasks are typically accomplished alone or sometimes with a backup officer. In rare occasions, if the task is too large or complex, they are assisted by special units made up of other officers, detectives, or supervisors. This makes it more difficult for officers to have full responsibility for proactive crime reduction.

Second, line officers and detectives become experts in the quick management of crime and disorder incidents in which they are involved. They may not be aware of what happens on other shifts or on days when they do not work. Typically, officers are neither encouraged nor rewarded to see broader patterns of crime. Thus, expanding the task structure of officers and detectives to manage larger-scale problems proactively and on a daily basis runs counter to their fundamental purpose. Often this results in more stress-relieving complaining than crime reduction and problem-solving accomplishments.

A confounding factor is that when officers are assigned to address problems, they are invariably asked to do so as part of their regular patrol or investigative duties. A patrol officer whose shift structure is organized around responding to citizen-generated calls for service typically drives around and proactively conducts subject and vehicle stops between calls and associated paperwork. It is not realistic to ask the patrol officer to carry out a large project in the middle of a shift when they might be prevented from carrying out these required activities.

To institutionalize proactive crime reduction, it is necessary to have everyone participate in the process. But how realistic is it to ask a line-level officer to fix a crime problem, such as a long-term hot spot of crime that has been occurring the last few years? Is the officer equipped to handle such a complex problem? Is it reasonable to require the officer to do so? When we assist agencies, we often hear from officers that it is impossible to be proactive and adequately address crime issues because they are too busy going "call-to-call." This will often be the first and main excuse they give as to why they cannot conduct proactive work. This will also be their rationale for resisting organizational change needed for crime reduction.

Yet, do officers have a valid argument why they cannot be proactive? We think they do, partially. That is, officers are not necessarily too busy and do have some time, but asking them to "do it all" is unrealistic. When crime reduction is relegated to line-level officers, they will often attempt to resolve complicated crime problems by redefining problems as incidents, making them immediately solvable.[2] They do this because they lack the requisite authority, resources, and time to conduct the types of analysis and responses that are necessary to bring about substantial improvements to a community-wide problem.

So officers, by the nature of their work, responsibilities, and position within the police organization, should not be the ones who are held accountable for proactively addressing crime problems. The importance of supervisory and command-level leadership in this process cannot be overstated. Their direct involvement is necessary to enact strategies that are shared and spread across ranks so the appropriate problems are assigned to the appropriate people.

Uncommitted Time Is an Important Resource for Crime Reduction

When it comes to developing processes and changing the culture to incorporate proactive crime reduction, there needs to be a candid discussion about "uncommitted time." We want to stress that there is invariably uncommitted time at each rank in each area of a police organization, and it can be difficult to address and change everyone's idea about uncommitted time. We consider uncommitted time a resource for crime reduction, and this is how an entire organization can be proactive. It is one of the most important cultural barriers to overcome to change a police organization from being reactive to proactive.

The common belief in police culture is that patrol officers, for the most part, do not have much uncommitted time during their shifts. In the many years we have worked in or with police agencies, we have heard this repeatedly from police officers all the way up to executives, in small, large, rural, suburban, and urban agencies. The common theme is officers are very busy and do not have time available during their shifts to conduct proactive work. When we have these discussions, we ask officers and sergeants their perceptions of uncommitted time and to rank between one and five how much they have on a typical shift (five being a lot of time). The common answer is either one or two, which essentially means they think patrol officers have none to very little uncommitted time. We have found this to be a fairly common belief among individuals at all levels of the organization about their own uncommitted time. So, clearly it is a common perception in police organizations that there is little to no time to be proactive.

There may be some truth to this belief during particular times of the day, days of the week, and seasons of the year, but there is a disconnect in the perception and reality of how much uncommitted time police have. Both research and our experience indicate patrol officers do have a discernible amount of uncommitted time. There are estimates from research studies that between 25 percent to 80 percent of patrol officers' time on a given day is uncommitted time. They conclude based on both quantitative analysis of CAD data and observations of officers on patrol, while some of this time is spent backing up other officers and writing reports, officers do spend a lot of their time waiting for something to happen.[3]

To fully address uncommitted time and to get the most out of the work-force, an agency has to address individuals' daily behavior. For example, an officer waits 15 minutes to go back in service after a call even though the call is over. Or, an officer(s) or even a supervisor(s) will show up to calls, as backup, when it is not necessary, or will stay on a call longer than needed. A very common example of an officer staying longer than needed is when dispatch contacts a supervisor about a pending call because no one is available. Once the supervisor advises dispatch that they will take it, usually an officer immediately goes back into service, cancels the supervisor, and takes the call. These are simple examples of how uncommitted time looks like assigned time.

The appearance of not having time applies to everyone else in the police organization—detectives, specialized units, civilians, and administration as well as each rank from supervisors to the executive staff. The behavior just looks a little different because most of these individuals are not tied to the radio and have more autonomy than patrol officers. We are not saying everyone does this every day, but everyone knows it happens, and it is part of the culture, which can leave individuals feeling as though they have little to no uncommitted time for proactive police work. But in reality, they do.

Therefore, changing the idea of uncommitted time is important, but it must be a change to the organization's culture not just to one person, one squad or one rank's behavior. For example, having one motivated patrol squad change how they use their time will not be enough to make the agency effective in reducing crime year to year. And it certainly would not be enough to institutionalize crime reduction strategies systematically. For example, if the patrol squad made up of a supervisor and five officers dedicated half an hour per shift to proactive crime reduction, it would amount to 3 hours of proactive patrol work per shift. However, if the same amount of time is dedicated by each person in an agency of 200 sworn (including all ranks), it would be 100 hours per day of proactive work. We know this is a simple example, but you can quickly see how fast shaving off a little bit of uncommitted time is a force multiplier and can be used to focus everyone in the organization on proactive work.

So, there is available uncommitted time, but it will take deliberate effort to overcome the culture, recover that time, and use it for crime reduction. It is an invaluable resource, and it costs nothing. However, new expectations for how people spend their time conducting proactive crime reduction should be realistic and coincide with the work people already do in their assignments. If the expectations are consistently implemented with clear processes across the organization, changing the cultural concept of uncommitted time can be done.

Crime Analysis Must Be Relevant for Crime Reduction

Each proactive policing approach that we know works is focused in some way, whether on places, problems, offenders, or the community. In both research and practice, there is no disputing that crime analysis plays a significant role in effective crime reduction.[4] However, crime analysis must be relevant and deemed essential by police for it to be used successfully.

Both our experience and research on the use of crime analysis by police indicates many agencies report having full-time crime analysts, but they have not fully integrated crime analysis.[5] For the leaders to just say crime analysis is important or to simply provide a wide range of analysis products to patrol is not enough to integrate crime analysis into day-to-day crime reduction operations. Police agencies have been able to operate without crime analysis in the past, so it will take more than a superficial endorsement from the executive staff and making crime analysis accessible for it to be used systematically.

In our many years of working with police conducting organizational evaluations, we have found similar results as those stated above. Many police personnel do not view crime analysis as a necessary component to reduce crime. In many cases, if the agency has crime analysts, their products are treated as optional—as a "resource" for officers. In addition, some police leaders have crime analysts and assume that their products assist police personnel to deploy crime reduction strategies; however, this is often not the case. We have found, in many situations, crime analysis products are not useful for crime reduction. This can lead to officers not trusting the analysis.

Another challenge is that police often think they know, without analysis, where and when to focus their proactive work. But studies have shown that officers to command-level personnel in both patrol and investigations are unable to consistently identify and/or are not accurate about where crime clusters are occurring.[6] For example, in a 2-year blind experiment we conducted testing the effectiveness of response to crime patterns, the crime analysts identified more than one hundred crime patterns that were not published for response (i.e., control cases). During that time, police identified three crime patterns on their own and were unaware the others were occurring.[7]

Some agencies invest in software that allows people to essentially be their own analysts. This software gives individuals access to crime data in their patrol cars or office computers to review past crime events and statistics. We have found that this approach, while it may be useful for providing information for situational awareness, is not effective in facilitating coordinated systematic crime reduction. It lacks the ability to create comprehensive analysis products that support an organizational approach and accountability that is needed to institutionalize proactive strategies. More effective is having trained crime analysts who create products that drive collective police action.

Police Accountability Is a Model for Crime Reduction Accountability

The police are accustomed to accountability in their day-to-day activities, and it is accepted that being a police officer comes with an enormous amount of responsibility and accountability. What other professions require employees to wear body cameras, be tracked by GPS, and have cameras in their cars? Police agencies deal with critical and high-liability situations on a regular basis, are responsible for responding to a large range of problematic situations in the community, and are accountable to the government and the citizens they serve. In addition to the laws police uphold, there are a significant number of rules, regulations, requirements, and policies that dictate police business.

Proactive crime reduction requires accountability to change behavior, but it is not easily accepted. When agency leaders start asking people to change their behavior to get more uncommitted time to do proactive work, there is often resistance and negative reaction associated with it. Something as simple as asking police officers to better manage their calls for service or administrators to better manage their administrative duties so more uncommitted time can be used for crime reduction is a challenge. The same can be true when asking officers to proactively patrol and get out of their cars to interact with the community or asking administrators to get out of their offices and proactively lead and engage in crime reduction work with the community.

We have found through our many interviews and observations of police that they feel there are often no clear-cut expectations for specific daily crime reduction work as there are for other police duties that have to be accomplished. Usually, the expectation is that certain individuals are asked to participate in crime reduction when they feel they have time, which most people believe they do not. This results in the perception that proactive work is optional. We have found this expectation to be true at all levels of the organization. Another theme we have seen is that accountability is not equally distributed across all ranks and individuals within ranks. People at certain levels of the organization feel they are being held accountable for crime reduction when others are not.

We have also found, after many years of working with agencies, accountability for crime reduction is not at the same level as it is for responding to calls for service, investigating crimes, and doing administrative work. That is, the same accountability police have for other processes has not yet translated to crime reduction. For example, it is not normal for patrol supervisors to write up officers for not conducting a proactive patrol or not getting out of their cars to proactively interact with citizens. But they will write up officers for not doing what they are supposed to in a call-for-service response. Thus, to truly change the organizational culture, crime reduction accountability needs to parallel existing police accountability to create both informal and formal expectations enforced through policies, a system for tracking activities, and mechanisms for ensuring they are getting done.

INSTITUTIONALIZING PROACTIVE
CRIME REDUCTION INTO POLICE CULTURE

To be successful in achieving sustainable crime reduction, it is necessary to both know what strategies work and how to overcome police culture in order to foster change. The term "institutionalize" is a word we use throughout this book, so what do we mean? It is establishing as normal or making something customary, expected, and accepted as part of an organization's day-to-day practice. Because implementing and coordinating multiple crime reduction strategies is sophisticated work, the planning and effort necessary to sustain them in a police organization can be easily underestimated. Since systematic proactive crime reduction is not yet an automatic process within the police operations, it requires a concerted effort to infuse it into police organizations and culture. Stratified Policing seeks to overcome these challenges while taking advantage of the strengths of police practice.

The primary purpose is to institutionalize proactive crime reduction into police operations following a similar model police use for "calls-for-service response." That is, the everyday process of responding to 9-1-1 calls is completely institutionalized into police practice and shared across American and international policing. This process incorporates many layers of rank involvement, and everyone in the police organization understands what needs to be done, what their role is, and what other people are expected to do. There are established expectations that everyone respects and both informal (peer-to-peer) and formal (supervisor-to-employee) accountability. Police often take for granted how much effort, innovation, organizational change, and leadership was necessary to get the process of responding to calls for service as efficient and normalized as it is today.

Many deliberate mechanisms and processes have been developed for calls-for-service response that include technology, policies and procedures, training, and a reward system, as well as clear practices for communication that reinforce expectations, resources, and accountability. These processes are sustained throughout the police hierarchal structure, formally through accountability and informally through the organizational culture. It does not matter what area of the community or the shift that patrol officers are working or the supervisors they are reporting to; there is an organizational expectation for all officers about how calls for service should be handled.

This system is more similar than it is different across police agencies, and there are profession-wide standards and consistent expectations by police, governments, and the community about how police should answer citizen-generated calls for service. We would argue this is why calls for service has been fully institutionalized and is sustained in practice. To illustrate the importance and how systematic this process is, the following is a breakdown of the mechanisms that ensure calls-for-service response is institutionalized:

- A comprehensive system of technology: Includes, but is not limited to, computer-aided dispatch systems, records management systems, in-car laptops, GPS, body cameras, radios.
- Policies and procedures: A high percentage of an agency's directives, standard operating procedures, policies, and memoranda dictate how officers should handle some aspect of calls-for-service response.
- Training: Police academy training, field training, and in-service training are all in one way or another related to effectively responding to calls for service.
- Resources: Includes sworn and civilian personnel, vehicles, bikes, boats, dogs, and equipment that support responses to calls for service.
- Award system: Most police awards are given based on an officer's actions during a call for service.
- Formal accountability: Most internal affairs investigations and discipline are related in some way to answering calls for service. An officer of any rank not properly handling an individual call for service can make its way up to the top of the chain of command for review and accountability.
- Informal accountability: Officers are quick to hold one another accountable for answering calls for service they are dispatched to (i.e., officers do not take kindly to answering someone else's call).
- Community accountability: The primary expectation of the community for the police is that officers respond when they call and are there when they need them.

Now, it is hard to argue responding to calls for service is not institutionalized in policing. It is also obvious that the process has evolved through significant time and effort, leadership, changes in expectations, and accountability, which all focus on making the process as efficient and effective as possible. The fact that this process is institutionalized and ingrained into the entire police profession can be illustrated in two simple examples. The first is that no matter if officers are sick or on vacation, if a sergeant is in training, if a commander is away at a leadership school for several months, or the chief is at a conference, calls for service are answered 24 hours a day and 7 days a week. This is because there is a system in place that anticipates absences, establishes processes, and ensures a certain level of response for every call, all the time.

As a second example, imagine that a 9-1-1 dispatcher gives a call to an officer, and the officer tells the dispatcher over the radio that they are simply "not in the mood" to respond. The reaction would be swift, since that behavior goes directly against police culture and processes that are institutionalized. Certainly, in this situation, supervisors, managers, and commanders would be extremely comfortable holding the officer accountable for not doing their job. That is if another officer did not beat them to it. In fact, this is so ingrained it is almost unimaginable that it would even happen.

Another important factor in the calls-for-service process is shared responsibility. Officers take care of the vast majority of calls for service alone or with the assistance of a fellow officer. Although most calls are handled properly, some require a supervisor's help. Fewer require manager involvement, and on rarer occasions commanders or higher get involved. Even though the calls-for-service process is carried out primarily by officers, to be successful, the entire system requires stratified responsibility and accountability. This approach requires other ranks to directly and physically assist by being on scene, coordinating efforts, making decisions, and taking, rather than delegating, responsibility for resolving the call successfully.

Even further, based on the seriousness and complexity of a call, the primary responsibility for assuring that the call for service is handled properly is pushed up the chain of command. Policies and established expectations determine how many officers and which ranks, units, or divisions should respond. These expectations are institutionalized to the point where response is not optional, there is little resistance, and the responses are collaborative to address a specific problem. For example, in most agencies, there is a policy that mandates two officers respond to a domestic violence call for service. A call for service, such as an armed robbery with injuries, often requires a supervisor and detective to respond. A call for service that results in more than two major crime scenes requires/expects a manager to be on the scene to make higher-level decisions and coordinate resources. A barricaded subject with a possible hostage situation requires a commander and several specialized units, such as SWAT and crisis negotiation. These are only a few examples, but it is easy to see how individual calls-for-service response is a shared as well as a stratified responsibility throughout the police organization.

In fact, this process is so ingrained and institutionalized that everyone knows when supervisors should be involved in a call and when they should not. For example, if an officer responded to a barking dog call and both the district manager and commander show up, the officer would think, "What the heck are they here for?" The officer would, most likely, tell other officers who would all be irritated. Actually, having managers and commanders show up to certain calls would be both counterproductive and inefficient to the calls-for-service process.

The main takeaway here is that calls-for-service response should be our model for institutionalizing organization-wide changes. When we look further into how calls-for-service response is actually carried out in police organizations, we see there are not only the organizational processes that support patrol officers in their response to calls, but there is also a stratified responsibility for calls for service. Higher ranks and additional resources become directly responsible and involved in calls-for-service response as the situations become larger and more complex. Thus, we contend that a set of processes and mechanisms as well as a stratification of shared responsibility should also be used to implement proactive crime reduction.

Consequently, Stratified Policing seeks to engage the entire police organization in the crime reduction process through a similar stratified and shared approach in a realistic way. That is, specific tasks that individuals will do are based on rank and assignment. Although line-level officers make up the majority of any police organization and will assist in all proactive strategies, they are not directly responsible for and do not lead crime reduction. Based on the complexity of the problem, both the responsibility and accountability to lead, coordinate, and physically carry out the strategies are shared and pushed up the chain of command similar to the calls-for-service process.

There are several reasons why stratification is effective for crime reduction. It ensures the proper people are involved, shared responsibility, more than officers are directly engaged, and more complex problems are the responsibility of higher ranks. In addition, those involved are tasked based on what is realistic and within the scope of their current day-to-day responsibilities. In other words, the current rank and responsibility of individuals within the organization determine the tasks each person completes, which build on and intersect with one another. Ultimately, what results is a comprehensive, multifaceted approach that is infused into established organizational practices. To reiterate, the goal of Stratified Policing is to institutionalize proactive crime reduction into police operations following a model similar to calls-for-service response—because it works! So, it makes sense to use a process for crime reduction similar to what police are accustomed to.

NOTES

1. Weisburd, D., and Majmundar, M. K. (Eds.) (2018). *Proactive policing: Effects on crime and communities.* Washington, DC: The National Academies Press.

2. Cordner, G. W., and Biebel, E. (2005). Problem-oriented policing in practice. *Criminology and Public Policy*, *4*(2), 155–80.

3. Lum, C., Koper, C. S., Wu, X., Johnson, W., and Stoltz, M. (2020). Examining the empirical realities of proactive policing through systematic observations and computer-aided dispatch data. *Police Quarterly*, 1–28. DOI: 10.1177/1098611119896081.

Famega, C. N., Frank, J., Mazerolle, L. (2005). Managing police patrol time: The role of supervisor directives. *Justice Quarterly*, *22*(4), 540–59.

Famega, C. N. (2005). Variation in officer downtime: A review of the research. *Policing: An International Journal of Police Strategy and Management*, *28*(3), 388–414.

4. Santos, R. B. (2014). The effectiveness of crime analysis for crime reduction: Cure or diagnosis? *Journal of Contemporary Criminal Justice*, *30*(2), 147–68.

5. Santos, R. B., and Taylor, B. (2014). The integration of crime analysis into police patrol work: Results from a national survey of law enforcement. *Policing: An International Journal of Police Strategies and Management*, *37*(3), 501–20.

6. Bichler, G., and Gaines, L. (2005). An examination of police officers' insights into problem identification and problem solving. *Crime and Delinquency*, *51*(1), 53–74.

McLaughlin, L., Johnson, S. D., Bowers, K. J., Birks, D. J., and Pease, K. (2006). Police perceptions of the long- and short-term spatial distribution of residential burglary. *International Journal of Police Science and Management*, *9*(2), 99–111.

Ratcliffe, J. H., and McCullagh, M. (2001). Chasing ghosts? Police perception of high crime areas. *British Journal of Criminology*, *41*, 330–41.

Santos, R. B., and Santos, R. G. (2020). Proactive police response in property crime micro-time hot spots: Results from a partially-blocked blind random control trial. *Journal of Quantitative Criminology*, 1–21. DOI 10.1007/s10940-020-09456-8.

7. Santos and Santos. Proactive police response in property crime micro-time hot spots.

Chapter Four

The Stratified Policing Model and Framework

Stratified Policing is an organizational model that includes a framework and specific processes to accomplish the institutionalization of a multidimensional set of evidence-based proactive crime reduction strategies. Once implemented and sustained, the model changes the organizational culture and incorporates proactive crime reduction into everyday operations that are organized, systematic, and fair in the distribution of work and responsibility. Ultimately, by implementing Stratified Policing, an agency can reduce crime by improving communication up, down, and across the organization, enhancing transparency, and establishing clear accountability for carrying out effective proactive crime reduction activities.[1]

Stratified Policing does not change hierarchical structure or individual job descriptions, nor does it create a specialized unit or rely on specific technology for implementation. Instead, it makes incremental changes to the activities of each person in every rank that are realistic and based on the established daily responsibilities of their assignments. It makes the most of the agency's current personnel, technology, and resources, which is vital for sustainability. What is asked of people is based on what is effective from practice and research as well as within the scope of their everyday work and responsibilities. Stratified Policing also infuses shared responsibility for crime reduction that requires everyone to do their small part of the larger coordinated framework. Thus, the model makes micro-level changes, which are much easier for individuals to adapt to. These smaller changes build on one another and result in macro-level organizational changes that are realistic and sustainable.

In its stratification of responsibility, Stratified Policing reestablishes patrol as the backbone of the organization. That is, over the years, it has become common practice that patrol takes a backseat to certain specialized units, divisions, and bureaus in crime reduction. The model centers crime reduction in patrol. Patrol managers and commanders carry most of the responsibility and are given the authority and resources to address problems. Other units, divisions, and bureaus support patrol's leadership. This is an essential principle in the model and dictates its specific processes.

Furthermore, Stratified Policing follows the calls-for-service process, which determines the complexity and priority of a call, as well as dictates who should respond, what actions should be taken based on assignments, and what rank should take the lead. The model is based on the complexity and priority of the crime problems police address at the immediate, short-term, and long-term levels. The model matches the level of problem with the stratification of ranks within the police organization to ensure expectations are realistically based on established roles and responsibilities. A structured framework and specific methods are laid out for each rank, crime analysis, appropriate crime reduction responses, and accountability by problem complexity. More specifically, Stratified Policing standardizes the creation and use of crime analysis products, outlines the types and implementation of crime reduction responses, and ensures accountability and communication at all levels of operations through day-to-day processes and a set of meetings.

In addition to infusing various proactive approaches, Stratified Policing processes encourage and foster coordinated and immediate response across ranks, units, and divisions in the organization. We offer a simple analogy that we call the Beehive Effect[2] as a way police organizations should react to assigned problems. That is, when threatened, bees respond by exiting the hive with enough resources (bees) to expel the threat and protect the colony. This is instinctual and happens every time. Not sparing any chance of failure, the hive does not send one or two bees to investigate the threat nor react days after it occurs. Instead, it responds immediately with a significant amount of effort. The bees respond with purpose, teamwork, and one goal in mind: to swarm and eradicate the threat. Finally, because this response happens every time there is a threat, everyone knows not to threaten a beehive.

Through the systematic processes at each level, the police organization has the same philosophy. When a problem is identified, it represents a threat to the community and, as a result, to the police. The Beehive Effect dictates police respond immediately to a problem consistently with an appropriate amount of resources and evidence-based responses to solve the problem. All divisions in the police organization respond cooperatively and based on their capabilities and function so a collective and comprehensive response occurs. The responses are automatic and institutionalized so much so that they become "instinctual."

Importantly, Stratified Policing provides mechanisms for the organization to change its current reactive crime reduction culture to a proactive culture through a distinct framework. Through implementation, an organization will institutionalize evidence-based strategies as part of "normal business" the same as a call for service already is. The model creates a structure that influences behavior so that the behavior can subsequently influence thinking, making the agency's overall crime reduction culture proactive.

The practical implementation of Stratified Policing within a police organization adheres to the model and its principles, but the framework will be specified based on an agency's organizational and rank structures as well as its capabilities and resources. However, no matter the execution every rank is responsible, proactively involved, and held accountable for continually engaging in proactive crime reduction work.

In order to operationalize Stratified Policing, the model is refined with a specific framework in which key components are defined, organized, and interrelated. Implementing change in a police organization can be difficult, and doing crime reduction correctly is multifaceted and complex. Accordingly, the framework's components have been developed deliberately through our work both inside and alongside police agencies of various sizes, crime levels, and jurisdictions. The purpose here is to distinguish and define the components, which include the following: (1) problem stratification, (2) problem-solving process, (3) evidence-based proactive strategies, (4) stratification of crime analysis, (5) stratification of responsibility for crime reduction, and (6) stratified structure of accountability. By the end of this chapter, Stratified Policing will be clearer in its structure. Subsequent chapters will provide further breakdowns of each level within the framework so the methods become real and provide an outline for concrete implementation and institutionalization of proactive crime reduction.

PROBLEM STRATIFICATION

Defining a system of problem stratification provides a structural foundation for Stratified Policing that organizes its framework. Since more than addressing individual crime and disorder incidents is necessary for proactive crime reduction, it is important to identify and respond to problems of different levels of complexity. Consequently, problems are distinguished to ensure the appropriate people are responsible for addressing problems that align with their job responsibilities, training, resources, and position in the organization. The framework begins with the idea that police address crime, disorder, and quality-of-life problems at a fixed number of levels that vary by their temporal nature and complexity. The framework specifies three levels of problems that include individual serious incidents (i.e., immediate problems), acute clusters of calls for service and crime (i.e., short-term problems), and chronic problem places and individuals (i.e., long-term problems).

Immediate Problems

Incidents are individual events an officer typically responds to or discovers while on patrol. They typically begin with citizen- or officer-generated calls for service and result in crime, disorder, or service-related tasks. They include such situations as disturbances, robberies in progress, burglaries, traffic accidents, subject stops, and traffic citations. Most incidents occur and are addressed within minutes and/or hours—most of the time within one shift. Police officers typically conduct the preliminary investigation. They respond to incidents with the goal of resolving each incident in accordance to the laws and policies of the jurisdiction and the police agency.

A proportion of incidents are deemed more serious by state laws, policies of the agency, and the community. Typically, detectives and specially trained personnel conduct more comprehensive investigations and respond with the goal of resolving the incident through arrest. Significant incidents represent the first level in the framework and are defined as a refined category of incidents. They are specific serious incidents that are identified by the agency as the highest priority because of their relationship to the agency's crime reduction goals, their seriousness, and community concerns. Examples include a violent robbery, shootings, home invasion, or residential burglary with a gun stolen. Stratified Policing employs a specific and deliberate system of accountability above and beyond normal operations. Higher levels in the organization ensure both the efficiency and effectiveness of the responses and ensure successful resolutions.

Short-Term Problems

There are two categories of short-term problems in the framework. They are considered short term because they usually occur over several days or weeks and correspondingly require short-term responses. The first is a cluster of disorder and quality-of-life issues manifested through citizen-generated calls for service, and the second is a group of crimes where offenders are preying on unsuspecting victims.

Repeat incidents are clusters of calls for service that represent problematic situations occurring at one location. They are usually made up of common noncriminal calls, such as disturbances, suspicious activity, alarms, problem juveniles, and domestic disputes. The individual calls for service that make up a repeat incident can happen within hours, days, and weeks of one another. The repeat incident is an important level in the framework, because much of what police address is related to disorder and quality-of-life issues that do not result in crime reports. If police can proactively identify and resolve repeat call situations before they become worse, time and resources can be saved and crimes can be prevented.

Crime patterns are groups of crimes that share key commonalities that make them notable and distinct from other crimes occurring at same time. They usually occur over several days or weeks. The commonalities can include MO, suspect description, proximity of the crimes in time and space, type of location, type of property taken, and victim characteristics. Crime patterns addressed by police normally involve commercial and street robbery, aggravated assault, rape, and sexual assault-related crimes (e.g., indecent exposure) between strangers as well as burglary, theft from vehicle, auto theft, and grand theft.

Because they are made up of crimes where offenders are preying on unsuspecting victims, crime patterns are considered vitally important to both the police and community as they are perceived as the most immediate threat to personal and community safety. The goal is to identify and respond to crime patterns quickly and stop additional related crimes in order to protect the community and prevent the crime patterns from becoming larger long-term problems.

Long-Term Problems

Long-term problems represent the final level of the framework and are the most complex. Generally, they are a set of related activity that occurs over several months, seasons, or years that stem from systematic opportunities created by everyday behavior in specific environments. Long-term problems can consist of common disorder activity (e.g., house parties, speeding in residential neighborhoods) as well as serious criminal activity (e.g., violent crime, drug activity). In contrast to short-term problems that are acute in their frequency and duration, long-term problems are chronic, stable over time, but may include acute spikes in activity. Long-term problems will contain numerous significant incidents, crime patterns, and repeat incidents. They require police resources in the short term as well as strategic responses that involve multiagency and community collaboration. Three types of long-term problems are differentiated in the framework.

First, problem offenders are individuals who have committed a disproportionate amount of crime and typically live in the jurisdiction. They move through different settings and take advantage of different victims and places. Because research shows offenders commit crimes near where they live, work, and frequent, the goal is to identify chronic offenders living in the jurisdiction and tailor the responses to their situations.

Second, problem locations are individual locations where there are concentrations of crime or problematic activity. These can be represented by one address—for example, a bar or convenience store—or multiple addresses that make up one collective location, such as an apartment complex, mobile home park, or a retail plaza. Within a problem location, various victims and offenders are involved in the activity, so it is the nature of the location that manifests the problem. The goal is to identify the most problematic locations in the jurisdiction and develop long-term solutions that reduce crime.

Third, problem areas are the most complex problem and are also called "hot spots" by police. Because in Stratified Policing there are both long-term and micro-time hot spots, the term "problem area" is used to avoid confusion. Problem areas are relatively small areas that have disproportionately more criminal and/or disorder activity than other areas within a jurisdiction. Problem areas are stable and persist over a long period of time and will contain significant incidents, crime patterns, repeat incidents, problem offenders, and problem locations. Problem areas are usually the most concerning to police and community because they have the most crime and disorder issues within the jurisdiction. The goal is to understand the underlying behaviors and opportunities creating the problem area and develop long-term solutions.

STRATIFIED POLICING
AND THE PROBLEM-SOLVING PROCESS

The problem-solving approach has been established as an effective method for proactively reducing crime.[3] These four steps of SARA guide all the processes in Stratified Policing:

- Scanning is identifying both small and large problems concerning to the public and the police, prioritizing those problems, and selecting problems for closer examination.
- Analysis is drawing conclusions about why the problem is occurring based on official data, observation, and experience.
- Response is based on the analysis results and includes identifying realistic responses appropriate to the scope of the problem and implementing them, which may require help from other agencies and the community.

- Assessment is determining if the responses to the problem worked, looking both at how they were implemented and their impact on the problem.

In Stratified Policing, the problem-solving process is not a special or deliberate exercise carried out for one problem at a time. It is fully integrated into the framework so the process occurs automatically. Those doing the work are not concerned with which step they are addressing, only that they are doing crime reduction. When they follow Stratified Policing methods, they are using the problem-solving process.

INTEGRATION OF
EVIDENCE-BASED PROACTIVE STRATEGIES

To be effective in proactive crime reduction, we know from the research that multiple strategies have to be employed and tailored. No one strategy solves all problems. Just as the problem-solving process is built into the framework, individuals do not consciously select a strategy to implement. Instead, they just do the work that is expected of them in Stratified Policing. The evidence-based proactive approaches are integrated into the framework so that they are realistic, efficient, and effective within the realities of police practice. The framework incorporates specific aspects of each approach:

- Place-based approach: Responses are implemented in both short-term (micro-time) and long-term areas as well as individual locations with disproportionate amounts of crime.
- Problem-solving approach: Problem-solving process is used, which incorporates immediate, short-, and long-term solutions.
- Person-focused approach: Responses are implemented for individual chronic offenders and field intelligence is used to support decision making.
- Community-based approach: Responses for every level engage the community in meaningful ways to promote trust and increase legitimacy of the police.
- Crime reduction accountability approach: A structure of meetings is used to systematically track responses, hold individuals accountable, and evaluate crime reduction efforts.
- Crime analysis: Systematic crime analysis activates evidence-based responses for every problem level and helps determine success.

While these are proactive strategies, the framework also incorporates traditional police responses and its established organizational structure. That is, many standard police responses can be used effectively in proactive policing as long as they are focused and not generally applied to all problem types.[4] Stratified Policing integrates long-standing police tactics, such as patrol, arrests, surveillance, offender contacts, and field interviews. In addition, the standard police organizational rank structure is the fundamental template for the stratification of responsibility and carrying out accountability.

STRATIFICATION AND THE ROLE OF CRIME ANALYSIS

Each proactive policing approach that we know works is focused in some way, whether on places, problems, people, or the community. In both the research and practice, experts agree the most effective way of identifying and understanding problems is to examine crime, calls for service, arrest, and other data systematically.[5] It is important that police do not rely on informal communication or individuals noticing a problem. The Stratified Policing framework is based on the calls-for-service response model, so something must activate a crime reduction response like the citizen activates police response with a call to 9-1-1.

It is the well-defined crime-analysis products that trigger a specific process at each problem level. Crime analysis is stratified in the framework by problem as well as by purpose. That is, for each level of problem different analysis products are required, and every product either is "action oriented" or "evaluation oriented." The crime analysis results either lead to a range of specific evidence-based responses or assess whether they are effective.

Even further, the role of crime analyst is vital as they become the "voice of the chief" and the "truth teller." It is not realistic for the chief to decide and assign each level of problem to different people in the agency on a consistent basis. So, using the agency goals, criteria, and processes set by the chief and executive staff, crime analysts dictate the day-to-day crime reduction efforts of the entire organization with specific analytical products. When crime analysis products are disseminated for crime reduction, individuals in the organization understand it is not crime analysts who decide what is important, but what they are getting is essentially identified and assigned to them by the chief. In terms of evaluation, because the chief also decides the criteria for success, crime analysis products establish what is working through ongoing monitoring of problems and evaluation statistics.

As the "truth tellers" of the agency, crime analysts identify, analyze, and evaluate problems without regard for who is being assigned a problem or what will happen if there is not a positive impact on the problem. Crime analysts being neutral and unbiased in their reporting is crucial for Stratified Policing to work. Some agencies implement crime reduction by having their commanders choose their own problems and then provide their own proof of success. In Stratified Policing, sworn personnel are assigned specific problems by the chief through crime analysts. On behalf of the chief, crime analysts provide specific products to better understand the problem and to determine if the responses are working.

STRATIFICATION OF CRIME
REDUCTION RESPONSIBILITY BY RANK

The framework stratifies immediate, short-, and long-term problems by the rank structure of the police organization. Doing this spreads the crime reduction work across the organization and creates realistic expectations for each rank in their contribution to crime reduction. No rank is excused from leading and actively working some aspect of proactive crime reduction. The complexity of the problems assigned matches the span of influence of each rank and the responsibilities of the assignment. The more complex the problem, the higher the rank that is responsible.

Police officers and detectives already have the responsibility of responding to calls for service and conducting investigations, so for short-term and long-term problems, supervisors, managers, and commanders are engaged by being assigned ownership of these more complex problems. That is not to say they do not have assistance from officers and lower ranks to carry out responses; however, they are required to respond themselves and are held accountable for their assigned problems and the effectiveness of the responses. Those at the executive level lead the accountability meetings, hold lower ranks accountable, and are held accountable for the overall effectiveness of the agency.

In addition, the stratification of responsibility can be compressed or expanded based on an agency's specific organizational structure. Larger organizations and those with more ranks will spread crime reduction responsibility wider and thinner to ensure everyone is involved. Those with fewer ranks must assign more responsibility to each rank. However, the most important aspect is that every rank in the organization is responsible, actively involved, and held accountable for an aspect of proactive crime reduction. Doing this ensures the processes are realistic and no one is overburdened.

Because police agencies have different levels of rank and may use different titles, the framework defines five general categories of stratification to denote the function of the various levels in the police hierarchy. These categories are used throughout the book. When an agency implements Stratified Policing, it will have to determine which specific rank does what, so we define each category and their corresponding responsibilities to guide this process:

- Officers/detectives: These are police officers, deputies, troopers, detectives, and investigators. Individuals in these positions, whether in patrol, investigations, or specialized units, are already assigned to respond to individual incidents, so they are not directly assigned the responsibility of resolving more complex problems. They are, however, held accountable for writing better police reports, conducting better investigations, collecting better intelligence in the field, and carrying out proactive crime reduction activities that are asked of them by their supervisors.
- Supervisors: This is typically a sergeant. Patrol supervisors are assigned repeat incidents, and investigations supervisors are assigned accountability for significant incidents. All supervisors carry out proactive activities asked of them by their managers.
- Managers: In most agencies, this is a lieutenant. Patrol managers are assigned crime patterns and problem locations. Investigations managers are assigned problem offenders. All managers carry out proactive activities asked of them by their commanders.
- Commanders: This position is responsible for overseeing the operations of a geographic area, division, or bureau and typically holds the rank of a captain. Patrol commanders are assigned problem areas as well as accountability for problem locations and short-term problems being addressed under their command. Investigations commanders are accountable for crime reduction activities carried out under their command. Other commanders carry out proactive activities as needed by the organization and support patrol.
- Executive Staff: These positions are at the top level of the organization and typically oversee multiple commanders and/or are second in command to the agency head for the entire organization. They are typically majors, assistant chiefs, deputy chiefs, lieutenant colonels, chief deputies, and under sheriffs. They are assigned responsibility for accountability of commanders and are held accountable by the chief for crime reduction activities conducted under their command. They lead the weekly agency-wide accountability meeting.
- Chief: We use the term chief to represent the agency head. But this also refers to sheriffs, colonels, directors, superintendents, and commissioners. The chief is assigned the agency's crime reduction goals and accountability for the entire organization's crime reduction efforts. The chief leads the monthly agency-wide accountability meeting.

Table 4.1 summarizes the assignment of problems and responsibility by category and function, which typically has to be tailored to an agency's hierarchy. The guiding principle for assignment should be making sure the rank assigned has enough authority to make decisions to adequately address the complexity of the assigned problem(s). A good rule is when an agency does not have all of these ranks, responsibility is assigned to a higher rank rather than a lower one. In addition, repeat incidents, crime patterns, problem locations, and problem areas should be assigned to patrol and significant incidents and problem offenders to investigations.

Table 4.1. Stratified Responsibility by Rank Category

Category	Ranks	Stratified Model Responsibility
Officer and Detective	Police officers, deputies, troopers, detectives, and investigators	Calls for service Investigations
Patrol Supervisor	Sergeant	Repeat incidents
Investigations Supervisor	Sergeant	Significant incidents
Patrol Manager	Lieutenant	Crime patterns Problem locations
Investigations Manager	Lieutenant	Problem offenders
Patrol Commander	Captain	Problem areas Crime reduction activities under their command
Investigations Commander	Captain	Crime reduction activities under their command
Executive Staff	Majors, assistant chiefs, deputy chiefs, lieutenant colonels, chief deputies, and under sheriffs	Crime reduction activities under their command
Chief	Chiefs, sheriffs, colonels, directors, superintendents, and commissioners	Agency's goals All crime reduction activities

Finally, an important point that can easily be overlooked is the allocation of administrative duties. Stratified Policing will require that supervisors, managers, and commanders be actively involved in proactive crime reduction. The chief should strongly consider how the current distribution of administrative tasks is carried out and be diligent in their equitable allocation. That is, in policing there is a tendency for executive staff and commanders to delegate their administrative responsibilities to their direct subordinates. The chief should ensure administrative responsibilities are distributed fairly and not simply pushed down to lower ranks since Stratified Policing requires more from commanders and managers day-to-day. For example, it is not reasonable to ask patrol managers to be responsible to lead and actively help solve crime patterns and problem locations, while at the same time do their own and some of a commander's administrative tasks. The same applies for commanders and executive staff. Ensuring that executive staff is assisting as much as possible administratively will allow those in their chain of command to focus more on proactive crime reduction.

STRATIFIED STRUCTURE OF ACCOUNTABILITY

Stratified Policing's structure of accountability recognizes meetings are necessary to systematically review the progress of crime reduction responses and evaluate the success at each problem level. A central objective of bringing people together to meet face to face is to regularly facilitate coordination and communication as well as reaffirm crime reduction priorities of the agency. The framework lays out a defined structure of daily, weekly, and monthly meetings. Since problems are specifically defined and assigned, the agency's expectations for crime reduction are established and transparent. Therefore, these meetings are purposeful and facilitate continuous responses and accountability. Each meeting feeds a higher-level meeting, and the structure ensures that the entire agency is working efficiently and effectively toward a common purpose.

Importantly, the chief's monthly meeting sets the expectations for all the work being done at lower levels. While the meetings feed the crime reduction results upward, by the nature of what the chief deems important in the monthly meeting and the ongoing results of the evaluation, the priorities and expectations dictate the focus in each lower-level meeting. Figure 4.1 illustrates the relationships among the different meeting levels as well as how crime reduction expectations flow down from the chief's monthly meeting and crime reduction work flows up.

Responses are discussed in daily roll calls as "missions of the day." Commanders in patrol and investigations have their own meetings to hold their supervisors and managers accountable and prepare themselves for the weekly agency-wide meeting. In that meeting, the executive staff ensures that commanders are resolving problems and coordinating with other units and divi-

Figure 4.1. Stratified Policing Accountability Structure.

sions. This prepares the commanders for the monthly agency-wide meeting where the chief holds the entire agency, but commanders directly, accountable and evaluates the agency's overall crime reduction efforts.

Ultimately, the purpose of the accountability structure is to create transparent mechanisms where accountability at each level ensures that individuals are doing their part in crime reduction. When responses are not effective, for whatever reason, problems are discussed at a higher-level meeting where higher ranks are engaged to provide additional resources and solutions as well as additional accountability. When this is done systematically, all levels of the organization are engaged and aware of the consequences so that all problems deemed important are addressed with the agency's full attention and capacity.

SUMMARY OF THE STRATIFIED POLICING FRAMEWORK

Figure 4.2 summarizes and illustrates the Stratified Policing framework and its components. At the bottom, systematic action-oriented and evaluation-oriented crime analysis products are stratified by the problems on the x-axis from left to right—immediate, short-term, and long-term problems. The y-axis contains the categories of rank and the lower diagonal line illustrates how problems are assigned in that lower ranks are responsible for immediate problems, middle ranks for short-term problems, and higher ranks for long-term problems. Below the line, the shaded area shows that evidence-based crime reduction strategies are implemented by all ranks where appropriate.

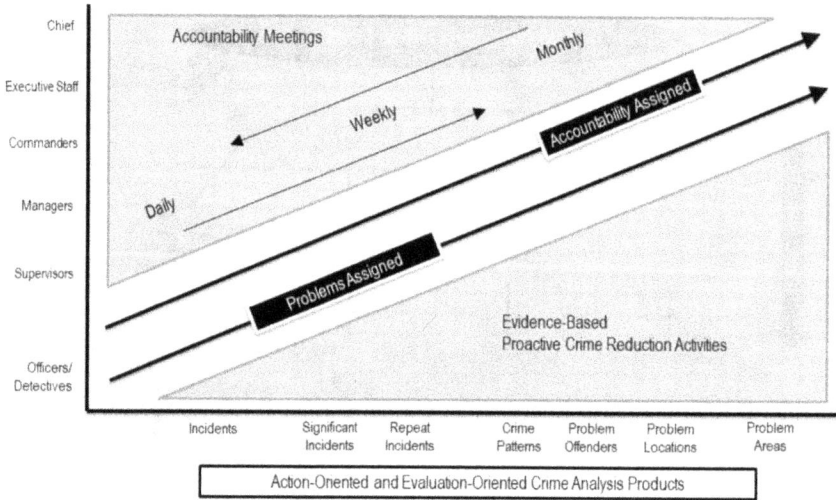

Figure 4.2. Stratified Policing Framework.

Based in the existing hierarchy of a police organization, ongoing accountability for crime reduction dictates that the rank above holds individuals accountable, which is represented in the upper diagonal line. Lastly, the upper shaded area represents the stratified structure of meetings by rank and illustrates how expectations flow down from the chief's monthly meeting and crime reduction work flows up from daily and weekly meetings.

NOTES

1. Santos, R. G. (2018). Police organizational change after implementing crime analysis and evidence-based strategies through stratified policing. *Policing: A Journal of Policy and Practice, 12*(3), 288–302.

2. Santos, R. G. (February 2011). Systematic pattern response strategy: Protecting the beehive. *FBI Law Enforcement Bulletin.* https://leb.fbi.gov/2011/february/systematic-pattern-response-strategy-protecting-the-beehive.

3. Weisburd, D., and Majmundar, M. K. (Eds.) (2018). *Proactive policing: Effects on crime and communities.* Washington, DC: The National Academies Press.

4. Telep, C. W., and Weisburd, D. (2012). What is known about the effectiveness of police practices in reducing crime and disorder? *Police Quarterly, 15*(4), 331–57.

5. Weisburd and Majmundar. *Proactive policing.*

Santos, R. B. (2014). The effectiveness of crime analysis for crime reduction: Cure or diagnosis? *Journal of Contemporary Criminal Justice, 30*(2), 147–68.

Chapter Five

Developing Crime Reduction Goals for Stratified Policing

Many police agencies develop crime reduction goals each year. At times, the goals are created superficially and can be vague and unrealistic. For example, when a goal is set to "reduce crime by 40 percent," it is not clear what exactly to focus on or how to achieve a 40 percent decrease. When this happens, the goal is often dismissed and never looked at again, and it is back to business as usual. It is important to set explicit crime reduction goals as part of Stratified Policing so efforts can be focused on specific problems prioritized by the agency. The more detailed the goal is, the more refined the methods to achieve the goal can be, and the higher the likelihood of achieving the goals. Just as individual calls for service are prioritized for response, goals provide a set of criteria so the agency can collectively prioritize strategies and create measures to assess success in reducing crime and disorder.

Since the purpose is to improve citizens' quality of life and safety, the community should be part of the goal development process. The selection of goals cannot be done as part of a simple administrative exercise (e.g., for accreditation purposes). Since the goals establish the direction and priorities as well as the internal and external expectations for the agency's efforts, the goal selection process requires deliberate thought and extensive amount of consideration. In essence, the chief sets the goals that become the charge for crime reduction, which spurs the organization into collective action. This is why the chief has to be very selective as a lot happens based on the goals.

Goals and crime statistics are important for measuring success; however, the purpose of setting them is not to simply watch the statistics change. The goals will be used to get everyone in the organization working toward a common purpose, provide transparency for the agency to the community, as well as prioritize and direct efforts. Evaluating the goals during the year keeps the organization focused and informs ongoing assessment that may lead to making adjustments to strategies. At the end of the year, they help determine the overall impact on the specific crimes being addressed.

The specific types of crime and disorder selected as goals depend on the jurisdiction and are based on the public safety problems that are most concerning to the community and the police. Although the goals vary by jurisdiction, the importance and process of goal development are the same. The main objective is to select crime reduction goals that are achievable in order to assist with getting everyone in the organization moving in the same direction. Consequently, in this chapter we discuss the purpose of developing specific goals and how they are developed. We also provide a process for specifying the goals so they can be measured, so expectations for responses are clear, and so both what the police do and the impact on problems can be evaluated in a straightforward way.

RESPONSIBILITY FOR CRIME REDUCTION GOALS

Stratified Policing begins and ends with crime reduction goals because they are a structured way to set priorities and measure impact of an agency's proactive efforts. The chief's responsibility is setting the goals, ensuring the entire organization is working to meet the goals through the various levels and responses, and then being held accountable by external entities (e.g., the city government and community) for achieving them. This task should not be delegated to patrol and investigations commanders by asking them to develop and send their goals up the chain of command. However, with input from the community and commanders, the chief and executive staff decide the goals and formalize them on behalf of the entire agency.

Through the ongoing processes of Stratified Policing, crime analysis products based on the goals determine where and when responses are focused; however, the entire organization works toward each goal collectively. Setting and evaluating progress on goals is the broadest level of evaluation in Stratified Policing. Each goal helps to prioritize problem identification and selection. Together the goals bring crime reduction efforts full circle through their evaluation and bookend the entire organizational process.

DEVELOPMENT OF CRIME REDUCTION GOALS

Crime reduction goals are different than the goals and objectives that are traditionally formulated in police agencies for 3- to 5-year strategic plans. They refer to specific desired results in reduction of crime and disorder that are the outcomes of proactive crime reduction strategies implemented by the entire organization. An agency's crime reduction goals are set to be fully evaluated and restated once a year. While there are no hard-and-fast rules about the length of time, this is a standard in both government and police practice. Many agencies set the year from January to December while others use a fiscal calendar to set goals (e.g., July to June or October to September). However, it may be more straightforward to use January to December since it corresponds to Uniform Crime Report (UCR) or National Incident Based Reporting System (NIBRS) reporting periods.

The goals are based on previous years' crime statistics, recent increases, concerns of the community, and other agency-specific considerations. In the Stratified Policing process, the goals are very deliberate, focused in their development, and prioritize crime reduction efforts. Everything cannot be a priority, so the number of goals is fairly limited. We recommend between four to six goals.

Chiefs should consider having goals both for crime as well as disorder (i.e., quality of life issues) since the different components of Stratified Policing focus on both types. For example, an agency with a large university in its jurisdiction may have goals for robbery and burglary but also for loud parties. In most situations, goals apply to the entire jurisdiction. Many jurisdictions that are a mix of rural and urban areas have different types and levels of crime in these areas. The crime analysis process determines where responses are best employed for each goal based on problem identification.

SPECIFYING CRIME REDUCTION GOALS

To make each crime reduction goal actionable and relevant for day-to-day operations, not only is the desired outcome of the goal specified, but so are the success indicators, baseline and target measurements, crime reduction strategies, and measurements of police response. This ensures responses or "outputs" (i.e., whether and how many strategies were implemented as intended) as well as impact or "outcomes" (i.e., whether the strategies affected crime and disorder) are assessed continuously. The following is a description of the six components that are specified when developing goals. The first component provides the "title" for consistent internal and external communication of the goal. The second, third, and fourth components are outcome parameters, and the fifth and sixth are output parameters. A variety of examples is provided at the end of the chapter for illustration of how these components can vary by crime and disorder type.

Crime and/or Disorder Goal

The name of the crime, disorder, or quality-of-life issue is essentially the goal's title and how it is referred to in written and oral communication within the agency throughout the year. A goal title does not name a general category of different crime types, such as violent crime, property crime, gun crime, or thefts. Instead, it names a specific type of activity—for example, shootings, street robbery, residential burglary, domestic violence, and traffic crashes. It is very important goals are explicit since Stratified Policing dictates which strategies are most appropriate based on the nature of the crime or disorder addressed.

Success Indicator(s)

This component translates the generally stated goal into a specific type of data that is measured and the level (i.e., percent decrease) the agency wishes to achieve. Because the goal itself is refined, general categories of UCR or NIBRS data do not suffice as success indicators. If the agency uses the general crime categories to measure responses to more specific crime problems, the true impact on the goal could be diluted. The success indicator also specifies the level of desired success. This is normally stated as a percent decrease. The number is a decision made by the chief based on previous crime levels and current long-term trends in crime in the jurisdiction and region, as well as what is realistic. Typically, agencies designate between 5 percent and 20 percent reductions for their goals.

We caution against selecting crime or disorder goals where the incident counts for a year are relatively low. In these situations, the percent change can be extreme and hard to explain. For example, one year an agency has ten crimes of one type and the next year five more; this is a 50 percent increase. While a chief would closely monitor the most serious, but low-frequency, crimes and report changes in counts, they are not good candidates as crime reduction goals.

Baseline Measure

The baseline measure component is the initial measurement of the success indicator(s), which is used to compare ongoing counts and to determine progress on achieving the goal throughout and at the end of the year. A specific value, typically a count of incidents, is listed along with the time period under consideration. Because goals are set and evaluated one year at a time, typically the baseline measure comes from the previous twelve months before the new goal period.

Depending on the circumstance, something other than the simple counts of incidents can be used for the baseline measure. For example, the previous year may have been unusually high or low compared to the previous years, so a baseline measure that reflects the average number of incidents over several recent years can be used. A jurisdiction that expects a significant increase in population may use a rate (crime per population) as the baseline. That is, with an increase in population, one might expect more, not less crime, but an agency that keeps the crime rate the same or lower after a significant increase in population can show success in its crime reduction efforts.

Target Measure

The target measure component reflects the actual value the agency is seeking to achieve with its goal. It is computed using the baseline measurement value and the percent reduction noted as the success indicator. For example, in a department seeking a 10 percent decrease in residential burglary with a baseline value of 400 residential burglaries, the target is 360. If the agency used a 3-year average of 419, the target is 377. Finally, if the agency used a burglary rate of 485 per 100,000 population for the baseline year, the target is 437 per 100,000 population. Once the target is set, crime analysts produce the appropriate statistic each month for ongoing evaluation. Chapter 10 illustrates a specific chart we recommend for checking in on the targets each month as part of the accountability process.

Stratified Proactive Crime Reduction Strategies

For each goal, multiple levels of problems are simultaneously addressed since each goal is a high priority, and a multifaceted response is most effective. To direct the organization, this component lists how the goals are addressed to make the crime reduction expectations for the organization clear and transparent. It may not be appropriate to respond to each goal at each problem level, and the strategies are designated based on the type of crime or disorder as well as which evidence-based strategies are most appropriate and realistic.

For example, a street robbery goal requires response to significant incidents, crime patterns, problem offenders, and problem areas. Repeat incidents are not appropriate since they address disorder and interpersonal disputes. Since street robberies occur outside and typically in publicly shared areas and not individual privately owned locations, problem locations are also not addressed.

On the other hand, a theft from vehicle goal includes crime patterns, problem offenders, problem locations (for commercial locations, apartment complexes), and problem areas (for residential areas and commercial parking lots). This goal does not include significant incidents, since thefts from vehicles typically do not rise to the level of a significant incident and do not require in-depth investigations. This goal also does not include repeat incidents, since thefts from vehicles are not disorder incidents or interpersonal disputes. Clearly stating what the organization addresses for each goal separately ensures the right strategies are used for the crime or disorder type, as well as creates expectations and transparency about who is responsible and centrally involved in addressing each goal.

Performance Indicators

Performance indicators are measures of the work product of proactive crime reduction—the "outputs" versus the "outcomes." It is very important to distinguish performance measures from the baseline/target measures to ensure the right types of data are evaluated for the right purpose. Performance indicators track how much work the organization is doing, for example, how many repeat incident locations, crime patterns, and long-term problems are assigned and addressed. They also measure specific activities done as part of the responses, such as directed patrol time, number of subject and vehicle stops, citizen contacts, offender checks, arrests, and cleared cases. Finally, they measure the rate of success for short-term and long-term problems, such as percent of repeat incidents, crime patterns, and long-term problems that were successfully resolved out of those that were assigned. Importantly, these measures do not indicate whether the agency has made an impact on crime or disorder, but they indicate whether the organization is implementing proactive strategies appropriately and efficiently.

Table 5.1 provides a summary of the crime reduction goal components, their meaning, and their application.

CRIME REDUCTION GOALS: PRACTICAL EXAMPLES

This section provides various crime reduction goal examples to assist with the development of an agency's specific goals. There are no set criteria for what the goals should be since they depend on the nature of the crime in a jurisdiction, previous statistical trends, community concerns, the agency's resources, and the local and regional environment. These examples show how there are similarities in the parameters across goals even when the types of crime or disorder activity are slightly different.

Table 5.1. Summary of Goal Components

Component	Description	Application
Crime and/or Disorder Goal	Title of the goal	General statement about crime or disorder
Success Indicator(s)	Measure of impact (outcome)	Type of crime/disorder data; percent reduction
Baseline Measure	Initial measurement of impact (outcome)	Statistics from previous year(s)
Target Measure	Desired level to achieve and time frame (outcome)	Goal number to achieve (or beat) in a year
Stratified Proactive Crime Reduction Strategies	Strategies for immediate, short-term, and/or long-term problems	Significant incidents, repeat incidents, crime patterns, problem areas, problem locations, and/or problem offenders
Performance Indicators	Measures of crime reduction activities implemented (outputs)	# problems assigned, % resolved, officer activities

Example 1: Street Robbery

Analysis of crime data for one year showed the jurisdiction had 200 reported street robberies, and in 20 percent (40 incidents), a gun was used. The chief decided the goal was a reduction of 15 percent for all street robberies for the coming year. The significant incident process requires additional resources for the accountability, so this agency prioritized the more violent, gun-related robberies because it could not afford to treat every robbery as a significant incident. This agency also addressed this goal through crime patterns in the short term, and problem offenders and problem areas in the long term. Repeat incident locations deal with disorder, so they were not addressed. Because these crimes occur in the street/public versus in businesses or homes, problem locations were not addressed either. Performance indicators measured officer and detective activities related to directed patrol, investigations, and offender-focused strategies.

Example 2: Residential Burglary

Burglaries in the city were steadily increasing the last few years, and there was an anticipation this trend would continue into the next year. The data showed burglaries occurred primarily at residences in both single family

Table 5.2.   Street Robbery Goal Parameters

Crime Reduction Goal	*Street Robbery*
Success Indicator(s)	Reduce street robbery by 15%
Baseline Measure	January to December: [Previous Year] Street robbery: 200
Target Measure	January to December: [Coming Year] Street robbery target: 170
Stratified Proactive Crime Reduction Strategies	Significant incidents (guns only); crime patterns, problem areas, problem offenders
Performance Indicators	# significant incidents assigned; % resolved # crime patterns assigned; % resolved # problem areas assigned; % resolved # problem offenders assigned; % resolved # arrests and case clearances Directed patrol time, subject stops, vehicle, stops, field information cards, citizen contacts, offender contacts

Table 5.3.   Residential Burglary Goal Parameters

Crime Reduction Goal	*Residential burglary*
Success Indicator(s)	Reduce residential burglary by 20%
Baseline Measures	January to December: [Previous Year] Residential burglaries: 500
Target Measure	January to December: [Coming Year] Residential burglary target: 400
Stratified Proactive Crime Reduction Strategies	Significant incidents (resident's home/firearms stolen), Crime patterns, problem locations (apartment communities), problem areas (residential neighborhoods), problem offenders
Performance Indicators	# significant incidents assigned; % resolved # crime patterns assigned; % resolved # problem locations assigned; % resolved # problem areas assigned; % resolved # problem offenders assigned; % resolved # arrests and case clearances Directed patrol time, subject stops, vehicle stops, field information cards, citizen contacts, offender contacts, property recovered

homes and apartment complexes. The chief decided on a goal of reducing residential burglaries by 20 percent in the coming year. Residential burglaries were addressed through crime patterns in the short term as well as problem offenders and problem areas in the long term. The chief designated residential burglaries in which the residents were home during the crime or firearms were stolen as significant incidents. Also, the analysis shows 85 percent of the residential burglaries occurred in Districts 1, 2, and 3 (versus Districts 4 and 5). The crime analyst identified most of the residential burglary problem offenders and problem areas in these districts. Performance indicators measured officer and detective activities related to directed patrol, investigations, and offender-focused strategies.

Example 3: Retail Theft Eastern District

Property crime in this jurisdiction had been steadily increasing the last few years, and there was an anticipation the trend would continue into the next year. The data showed the increases were mostly due to theft and more specifically, retail theft. There was a significant number of commercial retailers throughout the jurisdiction, but because of the nature of zoning and district boundaries, the Eastern District accounted for 90 percent of the retail theft crimes, so this goal only applied to this district while other districts were focusing on different goals. Further analysis showed of the twenty-five businesses in the Eastern District with retail thefts, three were responsible for 70 percent of the crime. Retail thefts were addressed through problem offenders and problem locations in the long term. The chief designated crimes in

Table 5.4. Retail Theft: Eastern District Goal Parameters near Here

Crime Reduction Goal	Retail Theft: Eastern District*
Success Indicator(s)	Reduce retail theft by 20% *Eastern District 90% of all retail theft
Baseline Measure	January to December: [Previous Year] Eastern District retail theft: 1,000
Target Measure	January to December: [Coming Year] Target: 800
Stratified Proactive Crime Reduction Strategies	Significant incidents (organized crime), problem locations, problem offenders
Performance Indicators	# significant incidents assigned; % resolved # problem locations assigned; % resolved # problem offenders assigned; % resolved # arrests and case clearances Directed patrol time, subject stops, vehicle stops, field information cards, offender contacts, property recovered

which the suspects were professional thieves (e.g., organized) as significant incidents. Performance indicators measured officer and detective activities related to directed patrol, investigations, and offender-focused strategies.

Example 4: Domestic Violence

Domestic violence had been identified as a concern by both the police and the community, not necessarily for its frequency, but because of the potential for very dangerous outcomes. The goal addressed both the potential of lower level disputes identified through repeat calls for service as well as crimes reported to the police. The agency treated all domestic-related felonies as significant incidents. In the short term, repeat incident locations were addressed, as the repeat calls are often noncriminal and can indicate potentially problematic situations that could lead to serious crimes. In the long term, problem offenders, and by proxy, repeat victims, were the focus for this goal. Specific performance indicators vary depending on the strategies employed, but typically, they fall into activities related to social services provided and to the criminal justice system.

Table 5.5.   Domestic Violence Goal Parameters

Crime Reduction Goal	*Domestic Violence*
Success Indicator(s)	Reduce domestic violence calls for service by 5% Reduce domestic-related repeat locations by 15% Reduce simple and aggravated domestic assaults by 10%
Baseline Measure	January to December [Previous Year] Domestic calls for service: 3,500 Domestic repeat locations with 3 calls or more: 250 Simple domestic assaults: 400 Aggravated domestic assaults: 150
Target Measure	January to December [Coming Year] Domestic violence call target: 3,325 Domestic violence repeat location target: 212 Simple domestic assault target: 360 Aggravated domestic assault target: 135
Stratified Proactive Crime Reduction Strategies	Significant incidents (felonies), repeat incident locations, problem offenders
Performance Indicators	# significant incidents assigned; % resolved # repeat incident locations assigned; % resolved # problem offenders assigned; % resolved # referrals, # and types of services provided # arrests, protective orders, prosecutions

Example 5: Disturbances at Vacation Rentals

The agency served a beach area where year-round families and individuals rent vacation homes one week at a time. There had been significant issues with disturbances and parties, and long-term residents were very concerned and vocal. Because the issues arise in the short term and are identified through calls for service, repeat incident locations were addressed. In the long term, problem offenders (i.e., property owners who consistently allow problematic renters) and problem locations (i.e., individual rentals that are responsible for a large percentage of the problem no matter who is staying there) were also addressed. The chief designated very serious violent incidents that occurred at these types of properties as significant incidents. Performance indicators measured officer and detective activities related to directed patrol, investigations, and loud party-related citations.

Table 5.6. Disturbances at Vacation Rentals Goal Parameters

Crime Reduction Goal	Disturbances at Vacation Rentals
Success Indicator	Reduce disturbance, loud noise, loud parties at short-term vacation rentals by 20%
Baseline Measure	January to December [Previous Year] Disturbance, loud noise/party calls at vacation rentals (only): 2,400
Target Measure	January to December [Coming Year] Disturbance, loud noise/party calls target: 1,920
Stratified Proactive Crime Reduction Strategies	Significant incidents (serious violent crime), repeat incident locations, problem locations, problem property owners
Performance Indicators	# significant incidents assigned; % resolved # repeat incident locations assigned; % resolved # problem locations assigned; % resolved # problem property owners assigned; % resolved # citations and arrests Directed patrol time, field information cards, citizen contacts, offender contacts

Example 6: Gun-Related Crime Downtown

The jurisdiction was seeing an overall increase of crimes involving guns in the relatively large downtown area, which included night clubs, restaurants, theaters, and professional sports venues over the last several years. The guns

Table 5.7.   Gun-Related Crime Downtown Goal Parameters

Crime Reduction Goal	Gun-Related Crime Downtown
Success Indicator	Reduce gun-related crimes in the downtown area by 20%
Baseline Measure	January to December: [Previous 3 Years] Robbery and assaults involving guns occurring downtown average: 100
Target Measure	January to December [Coming Year] Crime involving guns target: 80
Stratified Proactive Crime Reduction Strategies	Significant incidents (crime involving guns and serious injury), crime patterns, problem locations, problem offenders, problem areas
Performance Indicators	# significant incidents assigned; % resolved # crime patterns assigned; % resolved # problem locations assigned; % resolved # problem offenders assigned; % resolved # problem areas assigned; % resolved # gun recoveries # arrests and case clearances Directed patrol time, subject stops, vehicle stops, field information cards, citizen contacts, offender contacts

were identified in a variety of circumstances, and violent crime was primarily the result of robberies that occurred on the street and aggravated assaults by young male strangers or acquaintances as a result of gang affiliation. Proactive crime reduction for these crimes focused on significant incidents which, in this case, were violent incidents using guns resulting in significant injury. This goal was also addressed through crime patterns in the short term, and problem offenders, problem locations, and problem areas in the long term. Performance indicators measured officer and detective activities related to directed patrol, investigations, and offender-focused strategies.

CRIME REDUCTION GOAL ASSESSMENT PROCESS

Once the goals are developed and provided to everyone in the organization, the local government, and the community, proactive strategies are implemented as specified in each goal. Each month, success indicator statistics are prepared, so the chief can "check in" and see how the agency is progressing toward the goal as part of the monthly accountability meeting. The statistics related to the goals are used by the chief to get a sense of the progress and increase pressure on the day-to-day activities if targets are not being met. Because activities are reported out each month by problem type, performance measures are collated once a year for the chief to assess the agency's collective efforts addressing each goal. For example, the chief may look at the percentage of crime patterns successfully resolved for a street robbery goal along with the arrest/clearance rate for that crime.

We have seen agencies reduce crime significantly with Stratified Policing where target measures are achieved. When this happens, the continuation of significant reductions may become more difficult. At some point, it may be necessary to only require "maintenance" for a goal that reaches a newly established low. That is, a comprehensive approach requires solutions that solve crime problems by correcting the underlying root cause of these problems. Therefore, the goals require less effort to maintain as successes are achieved and the goals are met each year. It is often necessary to maintain a goal for several years and monitor it. In these cases, the success indicator would be set at the new low.

Doing this shows the agency that the type of activity is still very important and is being monitored. Proactive strategies would continue for immediate and short-term problems, so levels do not increase or lower-level problems evolve into larger problems. In this situation, when resources have to be prioritized throughout the year, other goals with specific reduction requirements would take precedence.

Chapter Six

Immediate Crime Reduction: Significant Incidents

In the Stratified Policing framework, significant incidents represent the problem type addressed at the immediate level and are crime incidents that are most concerning to police agencies and the communities they serve. They are defined as follows:

> A refined category of incidents that are specific serious incidents identified by the chief as the highest priority because of their relationship to the agency's crime reduction goals, their seriousness, and/or community concerns (e.g., a violent robbery, shootings, home invasion, residential burglary with a gun stolen).

In most situations, significant incidents align with the agency's goals to ensure this immediate level of activity is incorporated into the multifaceted response to each goal. That is, to be effective, an agency should respond to its goal crimes at the immediate, short-term, and long-term levels. What is defined as a significant incident varies by agency and is based on what is deemed important by the chief.

Significant incidents are crimes that result from calls for service and are, in most cases, investigated by detectives. So, the skills and knowledge needed to respond to them are already established through introductory and specialized training, police academies, and in-service training. Their responses are already institutionalized into daily investigative operations. However, linking the most serious or sensitive incidents to crime reduction goals and having a systematic accountability process to ensure they are paid "special" attention are generally not institutionalized into police practice. Stratified Policing lays out a process for significant incidents to make sure certain appropriate and timely responses are conducted by patrol officers who arrive first on the scene and detectives who follow through on the investigations.

The idea is once a particular crime is considered a significant incident, there is a new expectation for responses from everyone associated with the incident. It does not matter who responds to or investigates the incident, more is expected from each level. Once a goal is selected by the chief, it becomes the mission for the agency. It activates the organization into action to collectively address significant incidents that fall under the goal. At this point, everyone is aware that a particular crime incident is mandatorily scrutinized from the initial officer response to the conclusion of the investigation. Everyone has a vested interest in these incidents since they know their efforts contribute to the larger crime reduction goal. Their jobs and roles become more important, and they will be held accountable. This small change in organization practice (i.e., extra scrutiny of a few important cases) influences individuals' perspectives and can improve the quality of their work.

Importantly, this increased level of expectation for significant incidents is applied to everyone in the organization and not reserved for a specific unit or the high-performing employees who already achieve these expectations. So, the purpose of the significant incident process is to take something as routine as responding to a call for service and improve on the quality of work being done as an integral part of the agency's crime reduction approach. It would be great if this much attention and scrutiny were paid by everyone for every single incident. But with all the other tasks police do on a daily basis, the amount of time, effort, and accountability this would require is not reasonable or realistic. Just as calls for service are prioritized by type and assigned different intensity of responses, this process creates a similar system for the most serious, important, or concerning crimes to the agency, so even most basic tasks are important and verified. Asking everyone to work at a higher level within their normal duties for only certain incidents is realistic and easier to hold people accountable.

As noted earlier, certain responses and strategies for addressing serious incidents are currently institutionalized into police organizations. Thus, Stratified Policing employs a specific and deliberate system of accountability above and beyond normal operations so higher levels in the organization (e.g., command level) can ensure both the efficiency and effectiveness of the responses. The rest of the chapter lays out this process, which includes assigning organizational responsibility, identifying and prioritizing the significant incidents, and accountability.

ASSIGNED RESPONSIBILITY:
INVESTIGATIONS SUPERVISORS

Since significant incidents are almost always assigned to a detective or group of detectives, the criminal investigations division is assigned responsibility for significant incidents. The commander of investigations is ultimately re-sponsible for ensuring these cases are investigated in a timely and successful manner; however, neither the normal investigative process nor the chain of command change for Stratified Policing. Individual detectives are still as-signed responsibility for case investigations that occur on a daily basis.

Investigations supervisors typically do case reviews, but this may vary based on the agency or the individual supervisor. However, for significant incidents, supervisors are more involved and responsible for maintaining higher expectations of detectives for significant incident cases. The supervi-sors are also held accountable by the investigations manager who ensures investigative responses are adequately operationalized and coordinated. The manager reports to the investigations commander to make sure the entire chain of command in investigations is intimately engaged. The commander reports progress to the executive staff in weekly agency-wide meetings and to the chief in monthly agency-wide accountability meetings.

IDENTIFICATION, ANALYSIS, AND RESPONSE TO SIGNIFICANT INCIDENTS

The process of identifying significant incidents is very straightforward. At the outset of implementation, the agency's leadership develops specific criteria for designation based on the crime reduction goals, community priorities, as well as other concerns within the jurisdiction. The criteria vary by agency based on the size of the jurisdiction, crime levels, types of crimes, community concerns, and type of agency, among other considerations.

In any case, the criteria identify significant incidents that are the most seri-ous relative to other serious incidents handled by patrol and investigations. When deciding how many categories, the criteria should not result in too many significant incidents per day or per week, so the additional account-ability process carried out for these cases is realistic and does not result in too high of a workload for those involved. For example, in a jurisdiction with low levels of crime and not many robberies, the chief may want to select all robberies as significant incidents. However, in another jurisdiction with high levels of crime and robberies, the chief may choose only robberies that involve a gun.

An example of a complete set of criteria with goal crimes and other types of incidents comes from a department we worked with serving a population of 160,000. Its significant incident criteria include the following:

- Suspicious deaths
- Shootings

- Serious violent gang crime
- Violent stranger sex crimes, abductions
- Serious aggravated battery committed by strangers
- Residential burglaries w/ gun stolen (goal crime)
- Robbery (goal crime)

In this case, two types are related to goal crimes and the others are rare, but very serious incidents that are very concerning to both the police and the community. Residential burglaries are refined to only those with stolen guns, so the total number of significant incidents each week is manageable for the investigations section and the crime reduction process.

Once the criteria are developed, all incidents are reviewed each day by a designated person who prepares a significant incident report. Since crime analysts review police reports on a regular basis, we recommend crime analysts prepare the report. It is important that the person designated to review incidents is outside the investigations chain of command since that division is being held accountable for response. If investigations personnel decide which cases they are held accountable for, it undermines the intention to increase the accountability for these particular investigations.

The significant incident report is brief and to the point. It provides a summary of what happened taken from the initial report, when the crime occurred, and identifying information, such as case number, crime type, date/time, location, victims, suspect information, synopsis. A police report is already written for these incidents, and detectives produce supplemental reports that can be reviewed if necessary, so the significant incident report is an "executive" summary of these incidents. The report is disseminated to the chief and the executive staff who distribute it to their own personnel as necessary. Importantly, the chief will likely be alerted to some of these cases as they occur (i.e., 24 hours a day/7 days a week) depending on their seriousness. Because the Stratified Policing process is focused on the ongoing short- and longer-term responses, the significant incident report needs only to be published Monday through Friday, normal workdays.

Analysis and response to significant incidents are typically carried out within the investigations division. Specific techniques and strategies are not discussed here because they are already institutionalized into police operations. The process covered in the next section focuses on the heightened accountability required to ensure whatever responses are being implemented are done in a timely manner, appropriately, and effectively.

ASSESSMENT AND ACCOUNTABILITY

For significant incidents, accountability starts in patrol with the quality of officers' initial responses and their supervisors who ensure the response was appropriate and timely and approve their reports. Accountability continues with detectives who conduct the investigation and their supervisors who check in on the progress, help make decisions on how to proceed, and approve written supplemental reports. For example, an agency designates residential burglaries where guns were stolen as significant incidents for their residential burglary goal. The first responding officer is more motivated to thoroughly dust for latent prints; speak to homeowners, surrounding neighbors, and anyone who was possibly on the scene; get accurate phone numbers; collect any videos; and write a thorough initial police report. A supervisor may feel the need to be a bit more involved to help the officer and is more careful reviewing and approving the report to make sure all the necessary tasks were completed and documented properly. Once the crime is transferred to investigations, the detective is motivated to conduct a persistent and thorough follow-up investigation.

Similar to patrol, the detective and the investigations chain of command have a vested interest to ensure everything is being done in a timely way. Obviously, the process of transferring initial investigations to detectives is already institutionalized. However, once a crime is designated as a significant incident, accountability for the agency's current standards is intensified throughout the organization for those cases. Formal accountability for significant incidents is facilitated by the executive staff and chief who hold the investigations commander accountable for the progress and success of the investigations.

More specific and informal status updates of investigations for significant incidents occur within the investigations division among the detectives, supervisors, and managers. Updates in weekly and monthly agency-wide accountability meetings by the investigations commander verify the appropriateness and efficiency of the investigations, action items for the coming week or month, and effectiveness. This process is transparent since everyone is already aware of cases that are deemed to be significant from the onset of the initial call and what will be discussed. Therefore, expectations are realistic and allow the agency to prioritize resources to be effectively used for crime reduction goals as well as other specified crimes.

The main focus of this accountability is to make sure the executive staff and chief are comfortable with the types of responses implemented and whether they are executed effectively and in a timely manner. We have found when all ranks within patrol and investigations are equally concerned and focused on significant incidents, the quality and efficient progress of the investigations are greatly improved. In fact, we have also seen once the significant incident process is implemented, improvements to how non-significant incident cases are handled occur organically. One prominent example is that latent prints are recovered more consistently and videos are obtained more quickly across the organization for most crimes.

Assessment

The assessment process for significant incidents is the most straightforward of all the levels in Stratified Policing as it is the resolution of the case itself through arrest, exceptional clearance, or other means. It is the decision of the chief whether the significant incident is considered resolved, and when this happens, the significant incident is no longer discussed in any agency-wide meeting.

Accountability Meetings

Expectations for accountability meetings are transparent at the outset, and there are no surprises about which cases are discussed or what aspect of the case will be discussed. Since commanders must be engaged in this process, they do not rely on anyone else in the agency-wide meetings to discuss the particulars of the significant incident investigation. Their discussions of the cases are succinct and focus only on what was done in the investigation from the last meeting (i.e., not a review of the event itself and/or the entire investigation) and specifically what will be done before the next meeting. The following are the expectations for each type of meeting:

- Weekly Investigations Meeting: The investigations commander has an internal accountability meeting with investigations personnel to be engaged in the process and to ensure significant incidents cases are being done properly, which also helps the commander prepare for the weekly and monthly agency-wide meetings. This creates a system of communication and accountability that trickles down to managers, supervisors, and detectives overseeing and working the significant incident cases.
- Weekly Agency-Wide Meeting: The investigations commander speaks about all assigned and active significant incidents (no formal presentation) and covers the status of the investigations, what was done since the last

meeting, and the action items for the coming week. The commander is held accountable by the executive staff (e.g., assistant chief) to make sure the investigation is being done correctly and efficiently, and there is coordination among commanders throughout the organization when necessary. Lastly, it is the executive staff member's responsibility to make sure the commander is adequately prepared to be held accountable at the monthly agency-wide meeting. So, this weekly meeting is the opportunity for the executive staff to add action items and ensure the investigation is moving ahead adequately.

- Monthly Agency-Wide Meeting: The investigations commander gives a formal presentation on selected significant incidents, which includes the status of the investigation, what was done since the previous meeting, and the action items for the next month. The chief holds the commander accountable for the whole investigation. This is the opportunity for the chief to add action items as well as ensure the investigation is moving ahead adequately. It is ultimately the chief's decision about which significant incidents are presented each month. The chief might want to hear about all significant incident cases or only a select few. However, regardless of what is covered in the monthly meeting all designated significant incidents are discussed in the weekly agency-wide meeting. Significant incidents are discussed until they are resolved or until the chief decides they should be removed from the monthly agenda.

Documentation

The progress on each significant incident and its action items should be tracked in both the weekly and monthly agency-wide meetings. In the monthly agency-wide meeting, the investigations commander presents each case more formally to the chief using an electronic presentation. Emphasis is placed on brevity of both the presentation and discussion. The commander discusses information including a synopsis, the investigative responses that have taken place thus far, and action items for the coming month. For significant incidents discussed in several monthly meetings, there is no real need to discuss previous investigative responses since they have already been discussed and approved. The focus is on discussing whether the action items from the last month were completed, the new action items, and if there was a resolution to the case. After each meeting, the commander's presentation file is updated with any new action items that arise within the meeting itself, and is used to track the progress of the investigation at this level.

STRATIFIED POLICING
SIGNIFICANT INCIDENT PROCESS OVERVIEW

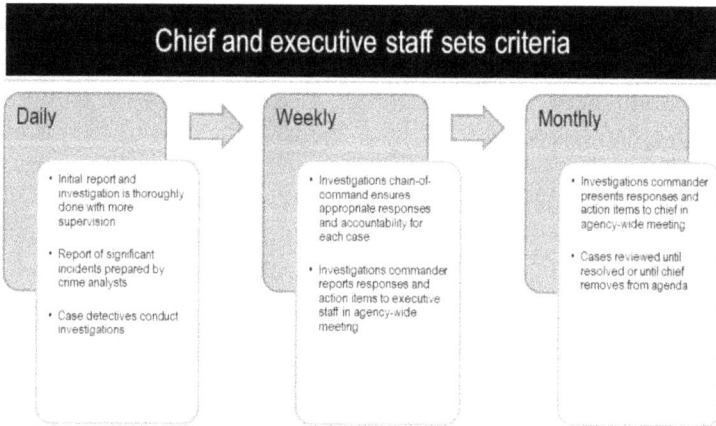

Chief and executive staff sets criteria

Daily

- Initial report and investigation is thoroughly done with more supervision
- Report of significant incidents prepared by crime analysts
- Case detectives conduct investigations

Weekly

- Investigations chain-of-command ensures appropriate responses and accountability for each case
- Investigations commander reports responses and action items to executive staff in agency-wide meeting

Monthly

- Investigations commander presents responses and action items to chief in agency-wide meeting
- Cases reviewed until resolved or until chief removes from agenda

Figure 6.1.   Significant Incident Process Overview.

Chapter Seven

Short-Term Crime Reduction: Repeat Incidents

Most police agencies focus their "crime reduction" strategies on crime. This, of course, makes sense. However, police officers typically write crime reports for only about a quarter of the citizen-generated calls for service they respond to, so this means citizens are calling the police about a lot more than just crime. To help a police organization be more effective in reducing crime and more efficient with limited resources, Stratified Policing systematizes identification, analysis, and response to repeat incidents, which are defined as follows:

> Continuously occurring citizen-generated calls for service that are similar in nature and happen at the same place. They are clusters of calls for service that represent problematic situations occurring at a location. Repeat incidents are usually made up of common noncriminal calls, such as disturbances, suspicious activity, alarms, and domestic disputes, as well as some interpersonal crimes when they are relevant. As short-term problems, individual calls for service that make up a repeat incident happen within hours, days, and weeks of one another.

Three main reasons for addressing repeat incidents are (1) to prevent a situation that appears to be minor from escalating into a crime, (2) to improve service to the community by resolving ongoing quality-of-life issues, and (3) to solve non-crime-related incidents so officers have more uncommitted time to conduct proactive work. As with all problems, the types of repeat incidents addressed should align with the agency's crime reduction goals, community concerns, and agency resources.

Any police officer can give many examples of responding to the same addresses multiple times for similar issues that were not crime related in a short time period. In fact, there are addresses officers continually go to for the same reason, day after day or week after week. There are just as many occasions when multiple officers respond to the same address at different times of the day and days of the week within several weeks without knowing other officers have been there. Oftentimes, if an officer did something different on the first or second call or knew other officers had been there before, the situation could have been resolved and additional calls prevented.

Furthermore, officers repeatedly face circumstances where there are several calls at a location in a short term that in the beginning are not serious but escalate quickly to a crime that may have been avoided. Domestic disputes and neighborhood disturbances are good examples where repeat calls can turn into much more serious situations. Importantly, when these do occur and the results are severe, the first question asked by the media and the community is how many times did the police respond and what did they do to prevent it.

In addition, there are times when one or multiple community members have a valid concern about a particular ongoing situation that affects their quality of life. This often results in repeated calls to 9-1-1 for assistance. If the police do not resolve the ongoing issue or work with the community toward an understanding of a possible resolution, citizens are left with the impression that police are not effective or do not care about their concerns. This can negatively affect the relationship and trust between the community and the police.

Since most of what patrol officers do, on a given day, is not directly related to crime, it makes sense to develop a process that identifies repeat incidents so they can be resolved, future calls at the locations can be prevented, and those resources can be allocated to crime reduction. For example, instead of allowing multiple officers to respond eight times to the same address in 3 weeks without any review or discussion, this process would identify the address as a repeat incident location after three calls. Once identified, the calls would be examined so that a better solution could be developed to stop future calls. This process results in officers having more uncommitted time that could be used for proactive crime reduction. Because repeat incidents occur frequently in jurisdictions, a process that does this systematically for a large number of repeat incidents over time has a multiplying effect on both increasing uncommitted patrol time, preventing serious crime, and increasing community satisfaction.

Consequently, Stratified Policing institutionalizes a problem-solving process for addressing repeat calls for service, which is an approach many agencies do not consider since they focus on one call for service at a time without looking at the totality of the situation. This is an important component of an agency's overall proactive approach, since it makes the organization more efficient and creates time to proactively respond to other crime reduction priorities. In addition, there is real potential for having an impact on certain types of serious crime and disorder that are likely to come to the attention of the police as noncriminal and interpersonal issues. The rest of the chapter lays out this process, which includes assigning responsibility, identifying and analyzing repeat incidents, responding, assessment, and accountability.

ASSIGNED RESPONSIBILITY: PATROL SUPERVISORS

Repeat incidents are assigned to patrol supervisors (e.g., sergeants). If geographically deployed, patrol supervisors are assigned repeat incidents occurring within their assigned areas. If not geographically deployed, they are assigned repeat incidents based on the time and nature of the issue and/or on an equal workload. All patrol supervisors, including those working midnight shift, are assigned repeat incidents because responses can be carried out various times of the day as well as evening hours.

One important component of Stratified Policing is engaging all ranks in crime reduction activities in realistic ways. It is reasonable this responsibility is assigned to patrol supervisors since repeat incidents are less complex, short-term problems that evolve out of supervisors' own patrol officers' activities. Supervisors are also better able than officers to carve out time to review, problem solve, and respond to repeat incidents during their shifts. Repeat incidents are not assigned to patrol officers because they have already responded to the individual calls for service that make up a repeat incident and were not able to resolve the issue.

By assigning the supervisors repeat incidents, mechanisms are created for improving responses to the types of citizen-generated calls for service prioritized by the agency. It becomes the job of the supervisors to determine why the officers were not able to resolve the ongoing issue and do something differently themselves. This process creates an incentive for supervisors to be more aware of each officer's ability and help officers improve their call for service responses. If officers are more effective, supervisors will have fewer repeat incidents to address. The process also creates an incentive for officers to communicate with one another and be aware of locations where multiple calls are starting to occur. If they know their own supervisor will be assigned work based on their inability to resolve a situation, they will do a better job. Few officers want to be the reason their supervisors are assigned more work, especially because this can also mean even higher ranks could get involved.

IDENTIFICATION AND ANALYSIS OF
REPEAT INCIDENT LOCATIONS

This process focuses on individual repeat incident locations as the unit of response. Not all repeat call situations are addressed. Agencies should be selective in how they utilize this process to ensure responses are meaningful and contribute to the agency's overall crime reduction approach and community concerns. Identification of repeat incident locations is fairly straightforward and occurs through a weekly report.

Criteria for the report are developed and approved by the chief with the goal to identify individual locations that have received multiple calls for service within a relatively short time period. Citizen-generated calls for service data (i.e., not officer-generated calls) are used to identify repeat incident locations because they represent calls for assistance from the community about quality-of-life issues, disorder, and interpersonal disputes.

Repeat Incident Location Criteria

In reality, there are many more repeat incident locations that occur than an agency can proactively address, so activity that aligns with the agency's priorities should be the focus. There are five criteria that must be determined and approved by the chief before a repeat incident report can be created. They include (1) geographic unit of analysis, (2) call types, (3) geography covered, (4) time period, and (5) threshold of citizen-generated calls for service per location.

1. Geographic unit of analysis. We recommend physical address as the unit of analysis for most repeat incident reports since most calls have a distinct address. This is particularly relevant for a report focusing on issues at residences, such as domestic violence. However, there are other factors to consider as well. The recorded address for a call for service does not always reflect where the problem is occurring, but could be where the call came from. The unit of analysis might be expanded to consider multiple addresses together, for example, in the case of apartment complexes or business plazas. For activity such as loud parties or narcotics-related disorder where calls may come in from multiple addresses near the problematic activity, the unit of analysis might be extended to street segments (i.e., street blocks).

2. Call types. Repeat incident locations are not locations with any type of call for service, but are addresses where similar types of calls are reoccurring that might indicate an ongoing issue. Calls for service types are relatively generic and may not accurately represent what actually happened on a call.

Often, broader call types are selected for the report so they encompass the type of issues the agency is focusing on with this process. An agency creates more than one type of report if distinctly different types of activity need to be addressed. The following are examples of different repeat incident location reports and call types that might be used:

- Domestic violence: Disturbance, urgent check welfare, domestic disturbance, domestic violence, fight, keep the peace, animal cruelty, harassment, violation of order, custody issue, stalking, abuse, neglect
- General disorder: Disturbance, check welfare, loitering, trespassing, neighbor trouble, juvenile trouble, loud noise, loud party, suspicious activity, narcotics activity, unwelcome subject
- Narcotics-related disorder: Suspicious person, suspicious vehicle, loitering, unwelcome subject, trespassing, narcotics activity, shots fired, weapons
- Loud parties: Loud noise, loud party, loud music, disturbance, fight, neighbor dispute, drunk in public
- Burglary alarms: Residential alarm, commercial alarm, general alarm
- Traffic crashes: Traffic crash-related calls

3. Geography covered by the report. Repeat incident locations are assigned to patrol supervisors, so the reports match their geographic deployment. That is, if they are assigned to districts, the report is produced for each district separately. If they are assigned by shift, the report covers the entire jurisdiction. In some cases, a report may be produced for only a smaller geographic area within the jurisdiction if specific activity occurs there predominantly. For example, we worked with an agency where the north side was primarily commercial, and the south side was residential. The agency produced a domestic violence repeat incident location report only for the south side.

4. Time period. We recommend the repeat incident location report be produced and disseminated only once a week and on the same day each week. We also recommend the report cover the previous 4 weeks (i.e., 28 days) from the day it was disseminated (i.e., "a rolling time period"). Doing this allows the report to be up to date each week and to show new calls at addresses that were previously on the report so it can be used for the assessment process, discussed later.

5. Threshold. An agency sets the minimum number of calls a location must have to be on the report. This is the most important criterion as it determines how many locations are assigned to supervisors each week. Thresholds can vary by different type of activity or by smaller patrol areas (e.g., district). The goal is to balance identifying locations as soon as possible with identifying a realistic number of new locations that are assigned to supervisors each week. Analysis of calls for service data is required to

determine the threshold. Because the report reflects a rolling time period, locations supervisors are already working will carry over. That is, after the first report, most of the locations on a report will not be new but already assigned. Before finalizing the threshold, multiple weeks of reports should be produced with different thresholds to evaluate how it changes the number of new locations each week. Agencies we have worked with have set thresholds as low as three and as high as seven calls. Typically, they start the process with three to four calls and adjust up or down as they implement and refine the process.

These are just guidelines, and the agency determines what is most appropriate. For example, some agencies start the process more conservatively with a higher threshold that produces fewer locations. As supervisors learn the process and are successful, the threshold is lowered. We have seen agencies that have institutionalized this process significantly reduce the threshold without increasing the number of locations. This was a result of officers being more aware of potential repeat incident locations and better addressing individual calls for service.

Report Format

The repeat incident location report is created by crime analysts and provides information about calls for service at each location. However, the report is limited based on the minimal descriptive data that is available about each call in the computer-aided dispatch system (CAD). The report includes the primary call information, including the incident number, the date and weekday of the call, the time the call was received, the call type, the disposition of the call, and the primary officer who responded.

Importantly, there may be locations that consistently have many more than the minimum threshold, so they are on the report each week. Many times, these are locations at which there is a lot of activity, but the calls do not necessarily represent a specific short-term issue. Some examples are schools, large box stores, and entertainment venues (e.g., theaters, bars, clubs). These locations would likely be the result of longer-term issues and could be deemed problem locations as described in chapter 9.

RESPONSE TO REPEAT INCIDENT LOCATIONS

Patrol supervisors conduct additional inquiries about the locations they are assigned. This is done to determine the true nature and potential cause of the activity to inform an immediate and tailored response. Supervisors may be familiar with the location, but it may be necessary to quickly examine both officer- and citizen-generated calls, talk to officers who have responded to the location, and/or go to the location just to speak to neighbors and observe. For example, a residence had five calls for service within ten days—one call for a family fight, two for a disturbance, and two for noise complaints. The calls occurred in the late afternoon and evening hours, but it is difficult to determine the underlying reason for the calls. The supervisor speaks with the officers who responded on different days and shifts, and then goes to the home to speak to the residents.

It is difficult to describe the specific responses that are implemented for repeat incidents because the situations that arise are varied and very specific to the environment of a location and interpersonal relationships. Some responses may be implemented simply by the supervisor and could be something as straightforward as a conversation with the involved parties to help them resolve the issue themselves. Repeat incident responses should focus on more permanent solutions than those implemented by officers for the individual calls, since those responses were not successful. Supervisors would likely engage other entities as necessary, for example, other divisions within the agency (e.g., traffic unit, animal control, and domestic violence unit), county social services, code enforcement, neighborhood associations, and business owners.

An agency might find over time certain repeat incident locations where the causes are similar require the same types of responses. In this situation, an agency might create a standard packet of potential resources for assistance (e.g., for domestic violence) or develop a specific process for handling the issue (e.g., the supervisor issues a nuisance citation after four loud party calls). Using these types of standardized responses ensures they are thorough, appropriate, and applied consistently across the jurisdiction by different supervisors. Time and consideration would go into developing these standardized responses, but they would save time in the long run if done for issues an agency deals with regularly in the repeat incident process.

ASSESSMENT AND ACCOUNTABILITY

The accountability process for repeat incidents includes systematically reviewing patrol supervisors' responses, documenting the work being done, and evaluating the success of the responses. Patrol managers (e.g., lieutenants) follow up each week with the supervisors who are assigned locations to ensure they are taking the lead in developing and implementing the responses in each situation. Importantly, responses are not to be delegated to officers, although they may help since the issue was not resolved at their level. The repeat incident process is a systematic way for supervisors to educate, hold accountable, and mentor their officers. This will help officers do be more effective at responding to calls and communicate with fellow officers to prevent locations from becoming repeat incidents.

Even further, similar to how unresolved calls become repeat incidents, this process also creates accountability for repeat incidents that are not resolved. If supervisors are not able to resolve a repeat incident location adequately and calls continue over an extended period of time, the location becomes a long-term problem. The long-term problem location is then assigned to the patrol manager who was responsible for holding that supervisor accountable. The manager is then tasked with actively resolving the problem location themselves as discussed in chapter 9.

In Stratified Policing, there are clear and transparent accountability processes that ensure good communication across the agency is occurring, and everyone plays their role and does their job. The agency sets criteria to determine when an unresolved repeat incident is also discussed at the weekly agency-wide meeting or becomes a long-term problem location.

Assessment

Assessment of repeat incident locations is focused, deliberate, and systematic. Also, the process of tracking and accountability is automatic, transparent, and shared with those in the chain of command who are responsible to address repeat incident locations. Crime analysts are responsible to produce the weekly report. Based on predetermined criteria, they examine whether repeat incidents are resolved, when they are to be discussed in a higher-level meeting, and when they become long-term problem locations.

To determine whether a repeat incident location is resolved successfully, an agency sets the number of weeks the assigned locations should be without another call for service. The weekly report already produced to identify repeat incident locations is used to assess the effectiveness of responses on a weekly basis. Each week the report covers the last 28 days so it shows any new calls at a repeat incident location that has been assigned. Again, the purpose of addressing repeat incident locations is to resolve the short-term recurring issues quickly and effectively to increase organizations' resources so more uncommitted time is available for crime reduction, and repeat incidents do not become long-term problems. Based on this, we recommend the time period for resolution be set at 2 weeks with no new calls.

When the repeat incident is not resolved within two weeks, there are two things to consider when determining whether response at the short-term level is not effective. These determine when a repeat incident location is automatically elevated for discussion and accountability at the weekly agency-wide meeting or to a problem location and assigned to the patrol manager:

- The first is determining how long repeat incident locations can be on the report before they are also reviewed at a higher level or designated as a higher-level problem. That is, while the location is considered resolved after 2 weeks with no calls, when it is not resolved, it is not realistic for the address to go immediately to the next level. We recommend that a reasonable period of time be allowed for two criteria that (1) pushes the repeat incident to the weekly agency-wide meeting discussion (e.g., 4 weeks on the report) and (2) determines when the repeat incident becomes a problem location (e.g., 8 weeks on the report).
- The second is determining how many separate times repeat incident locations can re-emerge in this process before they are also reviewed at a higher level or are designated as a higher-level problem. That is, while the supervisor may resolve the location within the two-week time period, it may come up again and again weeks or months later. The requirements for going to the next level should be realistic as well. We recommend the agency sets two criteria that (1) pushes it to the weekly agency-wide meeting (e.g., three separate times assigned and resolved in 6 months) and (2) determines when it becomes a problem location (e.g., six times in 12 months).

If either of these two scenarios occurs, further course of action is taken to resolve the repeat incident. The examples are just a guide and have to be adjusted based on the agency.

Accountability Meetings

Repeat incidents are incorporated into each level of the accountability structure based on the success of the response. If repeat incident locations are assigned and resolved within two weeks, they are only discussed between the patrol supervisor and manager. However, if they are unresolved or become long-term problems based on the agency's criteria, they are discussed in the weekly or monthly agency-wide meetings, respectively, where the patrol commander is responsible to present them. Similar to incentives created for calls not to become repeat incidents, and repeat incidents not to become problems, There are incentives and rewards to successfully resolve repeat incident locations at lower levels. The following is a description of the meetings and how they facilitate this process:

- Daily patrol briefings: Officers are made aware of repeat incident locations assigned to their supervisors. Supervisors are responsible for implementing responses, and they engage patrol officers to help respond as well as mentor and hold them accountable for improving their responses to individual calls.
- Weekly patrol meetings: Patrol managers report to commanders on repeat incident locations that are ongoing and may potentially meet the criteria to be discussed at the agency-wide meeting.
- Weekly agency-wide meetings: Patrol commanders present only those unresolved repeat incident locations that meet the criteria and discuss responses, action items, and results. The executive staff (e.g., assistant chief) holds the commanders accountable for repeat incident resolution and ensures the process is working within the patrol chain of command. The goal of accountability in this meeting is to keep the unresolved repeat incident location from becoming a long-term problem location. The crime analyst keeps track of the repeat incident locations discussed in this meeting and uses the criteria to automatically reclassify them as problem locations, when appropriate. When this happens, the location is taken off the weekly repeat incident report, and it becomes a problem location.
- Monthly agency-wide meetings: Patrol commanders discuss and are held accountable for only those repeat incidents that have become problem locations. Part of the first presentation of the problem location is providing the history of the location's repeat calls and unsuccessful responses. The chief holds the commander accountable on a monthly basis until the problem location is adequately resolved. Chapter 9 provides more detail about this process.

Documentation

Documentation for repeat incident responses that occur day to day should be done quickly and realistically. Individual patrol supervisors keep track of their own responses, and managers document however they think is appropriate to hold supervisors accountable. We recommend using an intranet system to assist supervisors and managers with this process as well as for accountability (discussed in chapter 10).

In the accountability process, documentation requirements become more formal as the repeat incidents move to the weekly agency-wide meeting. A repeat incident is discussed because it has not been resolved, so commanders give a synopsis of the situation, responses that have been implemented so far, potential reasons why it is not being resolved, and then action items for responses. In subsequent weeks, responses and action items are discussed until the repeat incident is resolved.

STRATIFIED POLICING
REPEAT INCIDENT PROCESS OVERVIEW

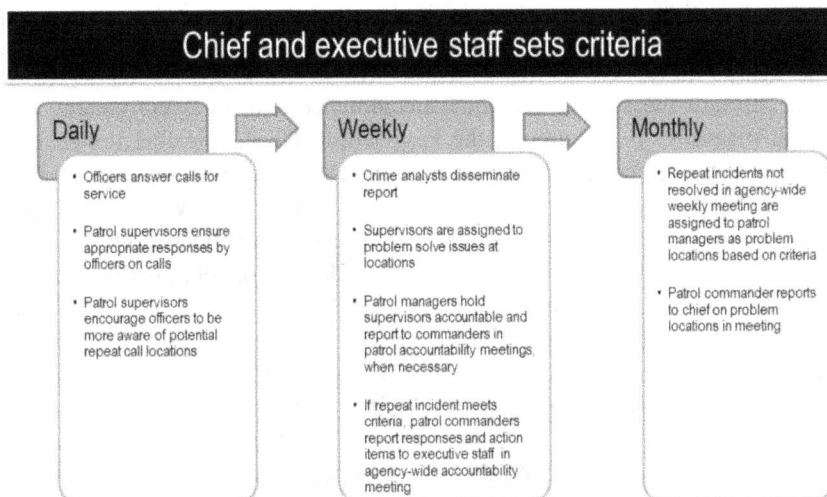

Chief and executive staff sets criteria

Daily
- Officers answer calls for service
- Patrol supervisors ensure appropriate responses by officers on calls
- Patrol supervisors encourage officers to be more aware of potential repeat call locations

Weekly
- Crime analysts disseminate report
- Supervisors are assigned to problem solve issues at locations
- Patrol managers hold supervisors accountable and report to commanders in patrol accountability meetings when necessary
- If repeat incident meets criteria, patrol commanders report responses and action items to executive staff in agency-wide accountability meeting

Monthly
- Repeat incidents not resolved in agency-wide weekly meeting are assigned to patrol managers as problem locations based on criteria
- Patrol commander reports to chief on problem locations in meeting

Figure 7.1. Repeat Incident Process Overview.

APPLYING THE REPEAT INCIDENT
PROCESS FOR DOMESTIC VIOLENCE

The repeat incident process described in this chapter provides a way to identify and appropriately respond to problematic domestic situations that have not yet risen to the level of a crime. Police are the gatekeepers to the criminal justice system and an integral part of the front line to prevent future acts of domestic violence and other forms of family violence in the home. How the police respond in a domestic violence call for service plays a fundamental role in connecting the victim, the offender, and other family members to needed services in most communities. The goal of using this process for domestic issues is to systematically provide alternative services in order to prevent the continuation of problematic behavior and/or its escalation to more severe physical violence or even death.

Overview of Domestic Violence and the Police

Given its prevalence, repeated nature, and dangerousness, domestic violence is an ongoing serious and costly issue for police. Domestic disputes or
domestic-related calls for service represent the single largest category of calls
for service for police and continue to be one of the most dangerous calls for
officers. Studies indicate domestic-related calls range from 15 to 50 percent
of all calls for service.[1] They account for the largest category of in-the-line-
of-duty deaths for officers in dispatched calls, representing an average of 14
percent of all officer deaths in a given year.[2]

Domestic violence also places a high demand on police resources as they
are personnel intensive—answering 9-1-1 calls, repeat calls to residences,
investigation time, and making arrests.[3] Offenders are often recidivists who
rotate through the system for domestic violence and other nonviolent and
violent offenses.[4] For example, the High Point, North Carolina Police Department found domestic violence accounted for a large portion of its violent
crime as well as was consistently the most frequent call type. These calls
required a minimum of a two-officer response and averaged 25 minutes per
call per person, which resulted in a total of 6,295 personnel hours committed
to strictly domestic violence calls in one year.[5]

The traditional police response to domestic violence has focused on making arrests to hold the offender accountable and keep the victim safe. After
several decades of mandatory arrest policies, there has been little decline in
rates of domestic violence and no change in number of domestic violence
calls, even though rates of other violent crimes have declined.[6] Although
some research shows arrest can reduce recidivism, there is a general consen-
sus that the current police responses relying primarily on arrest are not effective at reducing domestic violence overall.[7] Consequently, many researchers
and domestic violence professionals argue the solution is violence prevention
programs.[8]

Domestic Violence Repeat Incident Response

Domestic violence occurs in all jurisdictions, but most police agencies do
not have the resources to dedicate specialized personnel to domestic violence
cases, and proactive strategies to address pre-arrest situations have not been
adopted by many police agencies.[9] Another fundamental issue is that in order
for connections to community services to be made for domestic situations, the
police officer typically must make an arrest. When officers answer individual
calls for service where an arrest is not made, service connections are often not
made, especially if the situation is ambiguous and seemingly minor. When
multiple domestic-related calls, without arrests, occur in a relatively short

period of time, it could be an indicator of an escalating situation or additional problems that do, in fact, require services.

The Stratified Policing process for repeat incidents outlines a method for proactive response that can be directly applied to domestic disputes and interpersonal issues. This process facilitates alternative services that are systematically provided to help prevent future problematic behavior and/or its escalation to more severe violence or even death. Research shows the ability to intervene during earlier stages (not yet criminal) of emotional and verbal abuse and/or lower-level less physically injurious violence is critical to preventing future violence.[10] Thus, connecting victims to resources as early as possible is a worthy undertaking. Researchers find victims who work with advocates experience less violence, report higher quality of life and social support, and have less difficulty accessing community resources over time.[11]

The purpose of the repeat incident process is to infuse the work into day-to-day police practices. Thus, when used for domestic violence, it can be done within patrol without additional or specialized resources. In addition, the proactive nature of the process takes the direct responsibility from officers to identify repeat addresses themselves while on patrol. The weekly repeat incident location report identifies addresses with multiple domestic-related calls automatically. Patrol supervisors are assigned responsibility because they should be more experienced in handling people and working with community partners. They develop and implement the responses themselves, which will typically not be an arrest at this point. By becoming more involved with domestic violence crime prevention, supervisors can also mentor their officers to resolve individual domestic violence calls more effectively.

Lastly, there is a clear process of accountability for domestic repeat incidents that are not resolved, so unsuccessful responses can also be identified quickly and are assigned to a higher level in the organization. The repeat incident process does not replace what police and the criminal justice system already do for domestic violence crimes and victims, but provides a complementary strategy that fills the gap of dealing with lower level noncriminal calls. Police cannot prevent all of these situations from escalating, but this process provides a systematic and proactive way for police to do all that they can to address issues they become aware of through citizens' calls for help.

NOTES

1. Klein, A. R. (2009). *Practical implications of current domestic violence research: For law enforcement, prosecutors, and judges.* Washington, DC: US Department of Justice, National Institute of Justice.

Police Executive Research Forum [PERF]. (2015). Police improve response to domestic violence, but abuse often remains the "hidden crime." *Subject to Debate, 29 (1),* January/February. Retrieved July 31, 2020 from http://www.policeforum.org/ assests/docs/Subject_to_Debate/Debate2015/debate_2015_janfeb.pdf.

2. Breul, N., and Keith, M. (2016). Deadly calls and fatal encounters. *National Law Enforcement Memorial Fund.* Retrieved July 31, 2020 from www.nleomf/assets/ pdf/officer-safety/Primary-Research-Final-8-2-16.pdf.

3. Friday, P., Lord, V., Exum, M., and Hartman, J. (2006). *Evaluating the impact of a specialized domestic violence police unit* (Final Report No. NCJ 215916). Retrieved July 31, 2020 from https://www.ncjrs.gov/pdffiles1/nij/grants/215916.pdf.

4. Graves, K. N., Hunt, E. D., Sumner, M., Casterline, L., Fluegge, L., Varner, L., et al. (2011). *Applying a focused deterrence approach to domestic violence.* Greensboro: Center for Youth, Family, and Community Partnerships, University of North Carolina at Greensboro.

5. Sechrist, S. M., and Weil, J. D. (2018). Assessing the impact of a focused deterrence strategy to combat intimate partner domestic violence. *Violence against Women, 24,* 243–65.

6. Police Executive Research Forum. Police improve response to domestic violence.

7. Buzawa, E. S., Buzawa, C. G., and Stark, E. D. (2017). *Responding to domestic violence: The integration of criminal justice and human services.* Washington, DC: Sage.

8. Houston, C. (2014). How feminist theory became (criminal) law: Tracing the path to mandatory criminal intervention in domestic violence cases. *Michigan Journal of Gender and Law, 21*(2), 217–72.

9. Hirschel, D. (2008). *Domestic violence cases: What research shows about arrest and dual arrest rates.* (NIJ ePub). Retrieved July 31, 2020 from https://www. ncjrs.gov/pdffiles1/nij/222679.pdf.

Hirschel, D., Buzawa, E., Pattavina, A., and Faggiani, D. (2007). Domestic violence and mandatory arrest laws: To what extent do they influence police arrest decisions? *Journal of Criminal Law and Criminology, 98,* 255–98.

10. Buzawa, Buzawa, and Stark. *Responding to domestic violence.*

Campbell, J. C., Glass, N., Sharps, P. W., Laughon, K., and Bloom, T. (2007). Intimate partner homicide: Review and implications of research and policy. *Trauma, Violence, and Abuse, 8*(3), 246–69.

Campbell, J. C., Messing, J. T., and Williams, K. R. (2017). Prediction of homicide of and by battered women. In J. C. Campbell and J. T. Messing. (Eds.) *Assessing dangerousness: Domestic violence offenders and child abusers* (pp. 107–38). New York: Springer Publishing Company.

11. Sullivan, C. M. (2005). Interventions to address intimate partner violence: The current state of the field. In J. R. Lutzker. (Ed.) *Preventing violence: Research and evidence-based intervention strategies* (pp. 195–212). Atlanta: Centers for Disease Control and Prevention.

Chapter Eight

Short-Term Crime Reduction: Crime Patterns

Stratified Policing incorporates a systematic response for crime patterns, which are short-term crime flare-ups. They are defined as follows:

> A group of crimes that share key commonalities making them notable and distinct from other groups of crime occurring at same time. They usually occur over several days or weeks and commonalities can include MO, suspect description, proximity of the crimes in time and space, type of location, type of property taken, and victim characteristics.

It is important that an agency selects crime types for crime pattern identification and response that align with the agency's goals, community concerns, and agency resources. Crime types typically include commercial and street robbery, aggravated assault, rape, and sexual assault-related crimes (e.g., indecent exposure) between strangers as well as burglary, theft from vehicle, auto theft, and grand theft.

Crime patterns are dynamic, so it is difficult to anticipate when, where, and how a crime pattern will happen. Studies have shown that officers to command level personnel in both patrol and investigations are unable to consistently identify and/or are not accurate about where short-term crime clusters are occurring.[1] There are many reasons why this is the case. Since crime patterns can occur from one to several weeks, the nature of shiftwork and lack of internal communication make it difficult for officers to identify crime patterns and respond proactively. Crime patterns are much more than clusters of crime in an area. Therefore, they should not be identified by individual officers or supervisors with, for example, an interactive mapping program in their cars. Crime patterns are too important and concerning to the community not to have a systematic way to identify and respond with a multifaceted, coordinated approach.

There are four main reasons for addressing crime patterns: (1) to stop the immediate continuation of crime incidents during short-term crime flare-ups, (2) to prevent them so they do not manifest into long-term problems, (3) to help link and clear cases, and (4) to improve service to and collaboration with the community to resolve short-term ongoing crime issues. We liken the motivation for response to a crime pattern to that of responding to the common cold. While there are particular times of the year where colds are more common, exactly when a person will get a cold is difficult to predict. Once a person catches a cold, the symptoms get worse over a relatively short period of time.

Although there is no cure for a cold, experimental research shows zinc significantly lessens a cold's severity and shortens its duration.[2] However, zinc must be taken at the first sign of cold symptoms, and the dosage must be consistently taken for several days, which lessens the duration and severity of the cold. There is research showing similar results for crime patterns. To be effective in reducing and/or stopping future crimes in a crime pattern, there needs to be a quick and consistent response for a period of time as soon as the crime pattern is identified. When this is done, the crime pattern is both reduced in severity (i.e., number of additional crimes) and duration (i.e., length of time).[3]

The research on near repeat victimization supports addressing crime patterns as part of an agency's overall crime reduction efforts. Studies consistently show that when certain types of crime occur, more will likely occur close by soon after. They also find that near repeats occur in both long-term high-crime areas and in other lower crime areas.[4] The Stratified Policing process ensures crime patterns are quickly and systematically identified, and responses are properly coordinated, continuously tracked, and assessed. Importantly, through consistent response that slows down or stops additional crimes in each crime pattern, police can be effective in reducing overall crime levels in the jurisdiction. We have done research supporting this premise ourselves. So, in this chapter we cover both the crime pattern process and a brief overview of our research results.

ASSIGNED RESPONSIBILITY: PATROL MANAGERS

Crime patterns are assigned to patrol managers (e.g., lieutenants). If geographically deployed, patrol managers are assigned crime patterns in their areas. If not geographically deployed, they are assigned crime patterns based on the time and nature of the crimes or based on an equal workload. Patrol shift managers, including those working midnight shift, should be assigned crime patterns because responses can be carried out various times of the day, evening, and overnight. Although patrol managers utilize the appropriate resources throughout the organization, they are responsible to lead the effort, and their responsibilities should not be delegated.

There are several reasons patrol managers are assigned responsibility. Crime patterns are more complex problems and require more coordination and resources than repeat incidents. In addition, Stratified Policing seeks to engage different ranks, and patrol managers are better positioned within the patrol division to set aside the time it takes to lead crime pattern responses on a daily basis. Also, by their rank and job responsibilities, patrol managers have the necessary authority and autonomy within the organization to make decisions and coordinate resources across shifts and divisions. As part of their current duties, patrol managers already work collectively with other managers in patrol and other areas, which is required to be effective in crime pattern response. Consequently, patrol managers "own" each crime pattern assigned to them and are held accountable to ensure all of the required responses are occurring.

IDENTIFICATION AND ANALYSIS OF CRIME PATTERNS

While crime analysts have become very important in policing overall[5] in Stratified Policing, having dedicated crime analysts for crime pattern analysis is essential. Crime pattern analysis is not a task that can be automated but must be done nearly every day. There is an established crime pattern analysis methodology used by police crime analysts. The agency determines what crimes the analysts focus on, which should align with the agency's crime reduction goals, community concerns, and the agency's resources.

In crime analysis practice, there are a range of crime pattern types.[6] However, two types occur most often—series and micro-time hot spots. A *crime series* is a group of similar crimes thought to be committed by one person or a group of individuals working together. An example is four street robberies in a downtown area in which the same suspect threatens victims with a gun and demands their wallets. There are also series when there is not an identifiable suspect, but the crimes occur in such a short time frame and small geographic area that they most likely have been committed by one person or group of people. An example is seven thefts from vehicles along a residential street overnight. A *micro-time hot spot* is a group of crimes where one or more offenders prey on unsuspecting victims within a short period of time at locations that are close to one another (i.e., clusters of near repeats). An example is four daytime residential burglaries over the past 2 weeks in a three-block area.

Crime Pattern Bulletin Criteria

The agency should create detailed parameters, such as setting a minimum number of crimes and geography, that define a crime pattern. For example, crime patterns are identified as having at least two residential burglaries within a one-fourth-mile radius. Once a crime pattern is identified, crime analysts create a bulletin. It is both the identification and analysis product for the crime pattern process. Its purpose is to describe the crimes collectively, so that once published, police begin responding immediately. The bulletin is not merely a summary of all the information for the crimes, but is action-oriented and guides the agency's multifaceted responses. The bulletin also supports accountability mechanisms within the process.

It is important for a crime pattern bulletin to mobilize evidence-based responses and to quickly assess whether responses are working. Thus, it directly informs responses that encompass the four categories of effective proactive policing approaches:

- Place-based: Because crime clusters, the bulletin includes a map that depicts the area for focused response.
- Person-focused: Since offenders often commit crimes near where they live, the bulletin includes chronic offenders living in and near the area of response.
- Problem-solving process: The bulletin itself is the scanning and analysis that directs the response and assesses results.
- Community-based: The bulletin identifies a crime issue and provides specific information so that police can work directly with the community to resolve it.

The following are eight criteria that should be included when creating a crime pattern bulletin:

1. Bulletin Number: This is an identifying number with the year and a unique number (e.g., 2021-001, 2021-002). When new crimes occur in the crime pattern after the initial bulletin is published, the bulletin number is updated by adding a letter (e.g., 2021-001A). Multiple updates use letters in order to indicate the number of updates (e.g., B, C, D). For example, 2021-001C means three updates to the original bulletin.

2. Dates: Two specific dates are used to show when the bulletin is published and when it is updated. The publish date corresponds to the original bulletin number. It indicates when responses should have started. It can also be used to determine how long the analyst takes to identify and publish the bulletin by comparing it to the date of the most recent crime in the pattern. The second date corresponds with the date of the most recent update of the bulletin.

3. Title: The title contains pattern type, crime type(s), and general area of the crime pattern. It is used as a quick way for everyone to immediately know what it is about and to whom it should be assigned (e.g., street robbery series in district 1).

4. Summary Table: This table contains information based on all crimes in the pattern. Officers should be able to read through this quickly and understand how the crime pattern is different from other crime activity occurring at the time.

5. Offender Information: This is information and pictures of individuals who have been arrested or convicted of a related crime type and who live in or near the crime pattern area. These individuals are not suspects. They are listed on the bulletin because they may provide information about the crime or are worthy of additional follow-up. Crime analysts should ensure there is a practical reason the person is on the bulletin based on their level and type of previous criminal activity and where they live.

6. Field Intelligence: This includes field interview information collected by patrol officers and others about other criminal or suspicious activity that might be related to the crime pattern.

7. List of Crimes: This table contains information for each crime in the pattern, such as case number, date(s)/time(s), address, fingerprints and/or evidence collected, and unique MO information.

8. Map: The map illustrates the crime, known offender, and field intelligence locations as well as a circle with a radius measurement to indicate the geographic span of the crimes and potential areas of response.

Crime Pattern Bulletin Format

Figure 8.1 does not depict real police data and/or information and was created for illustration purposes. It depicts a crime pattern bulletin formatted with all the criteria as discussed. We recommend, when possible, bulletins be only one page. They should also have a standardized format, which helps crime analysts keep the information succinct and relevant. In this bulletin, there are four street robberies in a .23-mile radius in the Willow Neighborhood. The crimes occurred in the evenings throughout the week. There are three known

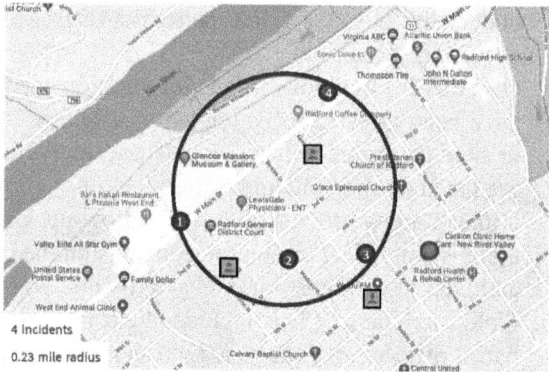

Figure 8.1. Crime Pattern Bulletin Example. Created with Bulletin Wizard by Smart-Force.

chronic offenders who live in or near the pattern area, and one FI that was taken after the bulletin was published. The bulletin has been active for a week (publish date July 12 and updated date July 19), and there have been two updates (i.e., "B"). That is, there were 2 crimes in the initial pattern within 2 days. One more crime occurred 4 days later to make it an "A," and then a fourth crime occurred 2 days after that making it a "B."

RESPONSE TO CRIME PATTERNS

The bulletin becomes the "call for service" that generates response. To initiate the crime pattern response, the bulletin is disseminated throughout the agency. We recommend doing this through an intranet system (see chapter 10), which is an effective tool for proper communication, coordination, tracking of responses, and accountability.

We recommend crime pattern responses be implemented immediately and for a minimum of 14 days from when the bulletin is distributed. This is based on our own research on micro-time hot spots[7] as well as near repeat research that finds 40 percent of near repeat crimes occur within 14 days.[8] For example, if a house is burglarized, another house close by has a very high likelihood of being burglarized within a short time period. This is why police responses to crime patterns need to be quickly coordinated, multifaceted, and realistic to carry out within daily police operations.

Importantly, crime analysts monitor each published crime pattern on a daily basis to determine if additional crimes that are related to the pattern have occurred within a 21-day period. If there are additional crimes, crime analysts immediately release an updated bulletin with the additional crime(s) information. When this happens, responses continue for a minimum of 14 more days (i.e., the response "clock" starts at 14 days again). Consequently, crime pattern responses are a minimum of 14 days but can last longer if additional crimes occur.

Research and practice have shown effective responses to short-term crime patterns consist primarily of strategies that police agencies currently use.[9] They include directed patrol, field contacts, contacting known offenders, surveillance, bait operations, investigative follow-up, and actively engaging with community members. There are a few very important considerations that we highlight about directed patrol implementation. The main objective of directed patrol is to deter offenders by being in the crime pattern area where offenders may live and/or frequently associate with others. Therefore, directed patrol should be implemented throughout the 24-hour period with emphasis on when the crimes in the crime pattern occur.

Those in patrol who are tasked to conduct directed patrol either by car, bike, and/or walking should be doing so in 10- to 20-minute intervals for as many times as possible during their shifts. Equally as important are the type and level of activity police do during their directed patrol. Officers must be active, and the more active they are the better. For example, officers should continually move about and when driving, get out of the car to interact with the community every time it is feasible. The duration, frequency, and type of activity are all important. Directed patrol must be done properly so that officers can create the greatest deterrent effect possible since offenders live and/or frequent areas where they commit crimes. This is why officers simply parking in the area writing reports or only very quickly driving through the area is neither desirable nor effective.[10]

While conducting direct patrol, police can also provide the community with a "watered down" version of the crime pattern bulletin that removes any details that jeopardize potential investigations. It has enough information for the community to know what is happening in the immediate area where they live. It should also include crime prevention advice for immediate implementation (e.g., lock doors and windows). Some agencies use community volunteers to pass out information to assist patrol. The important point is to actively engage with the community as much as possible, so they know why the police are there to help foster legitimacy for the concentrated police response. Additionally, citizens may be more inclined to help police by reporting something they see or a previous similar crime. They may also provide information that is helpful in resolving the crime pattern.

There are common police responses that the investigations division does as part of the multifaceted and coordinated response for crime patterns. Chronic known offenders living in the crime pattern area are included on a crime pattern bulletin when appropriate. Detectives should be tasked to contact these individuals. These responses are within the scope of responsibility and skills of what detectives already do. They are specifically trained in interviewing techniques and have the type of schedule that allows them to contact individuals at different times.

Known offenders listed on the bulletin are not suspects, but could be committing the crimes or know people who are since they live in the crime pattern area. The purpose of the contact is not necessarily to make an arrest, but is used to engage the person. The goal is to deter them or others and to solicit field intelligence. Detectives should also follow up on individuals listed on the bulletin who were identified through field contacts by patrol and others to help develop additional investigative leads. We cannot stress enough the importance of any offender-focused response being carried out in a manner that conveys its purpose to the community. The community should be aware the police are focusing their efforts on certain individuals and why, and not doing random and/or general sweeps in their neighborhoods.

There are other responses that the investigations division or other specialized units typically do that can be done for crime patterns. Since crime patterns are focused in areas, by day, and/or by times, certain responses are more practical and will result in successful outcomes more often. For example, the investigations division can support patrol's efforts by conducting unmarked surveillance. In addition, modern technology, such as static or movable surveillance cameras, can be used to observe certain areas of a crime pattern. Another example is setting up bait operations, such as placing a bait car in an auto theft or theft from vehicle crime pattern area.

Finally, responses to crime patterns can help detectives clear additional cases. For example, a crime pattern bulletin should be assigned to a detective who takes ownership and assists patrol's efforts. Simultaneously, the detective investigates the assigned crimes within the crime pattern looking at how, for example, fingerprints and evidence might cross over cases. This allows the detective to piece together information about the suspect, victims, and related information from the group of related cases instead of one case at a time. In situations when offenders are arrested, evidence, such as latent prints, can be cross-referenced with previous crimes that occurred in the crime pattern area.

For example, in one department we worked with, they created a process that when someone was arrested for a crime in a pattern, the crime analyst automatically went back 6 months to find all crime reports in the pattern area in which latent prints were unknown. As part of the automatic process, one of the crime scene investigators (latent print examiner) compared those unknowns to the person who was arrested. Doing this systematically for each crime pattern on a consistent basis resulted in a large number of cases that would likely not have been cleared without this process.

Although patrol officers make up the vast majority of those conducting directed patrol, it is important that all who are assigned to patrol, for example, K-9, traffic, and crime prevention officers, assist in the coordinated response. Criminal investigations, special investigations, and other support functions also play their role, so there is continuous police presence and responses consistently implemented for crime patterns. To institutionalize crime reduction into everyone's day-to-day missions, it is important that everyone plays their part. In Stratified Policing, crime pattern response is not tasked to only a certain group of officers. It is essential that everyone's "uncommitted time" is used in a coordinated way. When many individuals contribute a realistic amount of focused time, their responses become a large comprehensive effort.

Importantly, not all of these responses are appropriate for every crime pattern. It is the responsibility of the patrol manager assigned to the individual crime pattern to ensure appropriate responses are being implemented and coordinate them. The combination and intensity of responses depends on the nature and seriousness of the specific crime pattern, other crime patterns occurring across the jurisdiction, and available resources. We have seen in many agencies as well as in our research that when everyone does their part in a coordinated way, the organization is very successful in reducing crime, clears more cases, and helps the citizens feel better about police actions in their community.

ASSESSMENT AND ACCOUNTABILITY

The accountability process for crime patterns includes systematically reviewing the responses, documenting the work being done, and evaluating the success of the responses. Patrol managers not only are assigned but also take the lead in operationalizing responses for each crime pattern. Patrol commanders follow up each week with the patrol managers they oversee. Importantly, supervisors, officers, and detectives carry out the responses, but patrol managers coordinate their efforts and ensure the proper responses are taking place. They should not delegate this responsibility.

Again, the purpose of responding to crime patterns is to stop additional crime incidents and prevent crime patterns from reoccurring and manifesting into long-term problem areas. Therefore, if patrol managers are not able to resolve crime patterns adequately, the patrol commander also automatically has to discuss and is held accountable for the crime pattern in the monthly agency-wide meeting. Or, if multiple crime patterns occur in the same area over an extended period of time, the area can become a long-term problem area. When this occurs, the problem area is automatically assigned to a patrol commander to actively resolve and discuss in the monthly agency-wide meetings. This process of assessment and accountability is systematized to incentivize those who are assigned the crime pattern (e.g., lieutenant) and who supervise them (e.g., captain) to address crime patterns properly. This is an extremely important facet of the accountability process.

Assessment

Assessment of success for crime pattern response is a straightforward process. It entails systematically reviewing real-time implementation of responses and evaluating the overall effort by the agency. The process of tracking, accountability, and assessing crime patterns is automatic, transparent, and shared with those in the chain of command who are responsible to assist with crime patterns. Crime analysts are responsible to produce and track ongoing activity in the assigned crime patterns. The patrol manager assesses everyone's efforts to ensure responses are adequate for a particular crime pattern. We recommend an intranet system that allows a realistic way to track responses, improve communication, and help in the transparency of the process. Patterns are considered successfully completed if there are no crimes for at least

21 continuous days. However, if a crime pattern experiences an additional crime(s) within 21 days, as discussed earlier, crime analysts automatically update the bulletin by adding a letter (e.g., 2020-001A) and distribute it.

The goal is to stop crimes in the crime pattern as soon as it is identified. Therefore, the accountability process incentivizes every level of the organization to quickly resolve the crime pattern before it is automatically assigned to a higher level of accountability. There are clear and transparent accountability processes for crime patterns that ensure good communication across the agency is occurring, and that everyone plays their role and does their job. Similar to the repeat incident process, the agency sets criteria to determine when an unresolved crime pattern is automatically discussed in the weekly and then the monthly agency-wide meetings.

Updates to the bulletins indicate the responses are not resolving the crime patterns, so agencies set particular letters indicating a certain number of updates as the criteria. For example, one agency we worked with dictated that when a bulletin was updated with an "A," it is discussed in the weekly agency-wide meeting and a "B" in both the weekly and monthly meetings. Another agency set the criteria at "B" and "D," respectively, because they had a lot of crime patterns occurring at the same time and needed to manage the amount of time spent on patterns in the meetings. In any event, the number of updates that determine when a crime pattern is also discussed at higher-level meetings varies by jurisdiction based on unique considerations for each agency.

Accountability Meetings

Crime patterns are incorporated into each level of the accountability structure based on the success of the response. That is, if crime patterns are assigned and resolved within 21 days, they are only discussed in the patrol meetings. However, if they are updated one or more times or become long-term problems based on the agency's criteria, they are pushed to the weekly and monthly agency-wide meeting, respectively. The following is a description of the meetings and how they facilitate this process:

- Daily patrol briefings: Supervisors discuss ongoing crime patterns with officers and responses they are to carry out for the day for active patterns. These conversations change the nature and purpose of the briefings to become more focused on crime reduction. This process reinforces communication, expectations, and accountability among officers and supervisors. Even further, detectives or others attend the patrol briefings when necessary to discuss a particular crime pattern they are working on and either share or solicit information from the officers.

- Weekly patrol meetings: When geographically deployed, the area commander and managers discuss all active and recently resolved crime patterns. When not geographically deployed, these meetings cover the entire jurisdiction. In either case, patrol commanders ensure managers are leading and coordinating responses appropriately and that they are being assisted by support divisions. When a crime pattern is resolved in 21 days, no other review is required. However, when crime patterns are updated to a particular letter determined by the chief (e.g., "A," which is one update), they are also automatically discussed in the weekly agency-wide meeting by the patrol commander who is held accountable.
- Weekly agency-wide meetings: Patrol commanders discuss only those crime patterns that have not been adequately resolved. Executive staff (e.g., assistant chief) holds patrol commanders accountable for responding appropriately, and there is coordination among all commanders who should be contributing to the responses. Patrol commanders discuss responses from the current week as well as action items for the next. They are also responsible for talking about what criminal investigations or other division/units are doing for the crime patterns. Support commanders may contribute to the conversation as part of the collaborative process and coordination of crime pattern responses. However, since patrol commanders are ultimately responsible, they lead the discussion.

  The goal is to resolve the crime pattern, so for this meeting if there are no more crimes after 21 days (after the last crime in the pattern), no additional review is required. However, the agency sets a second criterion (e.g., bulletin with a "B," which is two updates), which indicates the crime pattern has not been resolved in two levels of accountability. When this happens, the crime pattern is also automatically discussed in the monthly meeting where the patrol commander is held accountable.
- Monthly agency-wide meetings: Patrol commanders cover only unresolved crime patterns based on the second criterion set by the agency. At this level, they make a formal presentation to the chief discussing crime pattern responses already implemented, why the responses may not be working, action items, and results. Patrol commanders are held accountable by the chief and discuss new information each month as well as what criminal investigations or other division/units are doing to assist in response. Again, support commanders may contribute to the conversation and are not responsible for reporting out on the crime pattern; however, the chief holds them accountable for providing patrol the assistance it requires. If the crime pattern persists after a certain amount of time, the chief might reassign the crime pattern as a long-term problem (see chapter 9).

Documentation

Because crime pattern responses are comprehensive and may involve multiple areas of the agency, real-time documentation is important at the operational level. It allows patrol managers assigned crime patterns to see what is being employed and by whom (e.g., directed patrol and offender checks by investigations). They hold individuals in patrol accountable for their responses and communicate with their peers throughout the agency to ensure proper responses from other units/divisions/bureaus are being deployed. Documentation should not be lengthy or cumbersome. It should be quick and realistic within the normal duties of officers, supervisors, managers, and so on. We recommend using an intranet system to assist in the process and have seen agencies implement them successfully.

In accountability meetings, documentation requirements become more formal as crime patterns are also discussed in a higher-level meeting. In weekly meetings, crime pattern responses are tracked systematically and efficiently so when necessary, the documentation can be used for the monthly agency-wide meeting. In the monthly agency-wide meeting, the patrol commander gives an electronic formal presentation about each crime pattern that has met the criteria. Chapter 10 provides a more detailed description of how an intranet system is used for accountability and reporting.

STRATIFIED POLICING
CRIME PATTERN PROCESS OVERVIEW

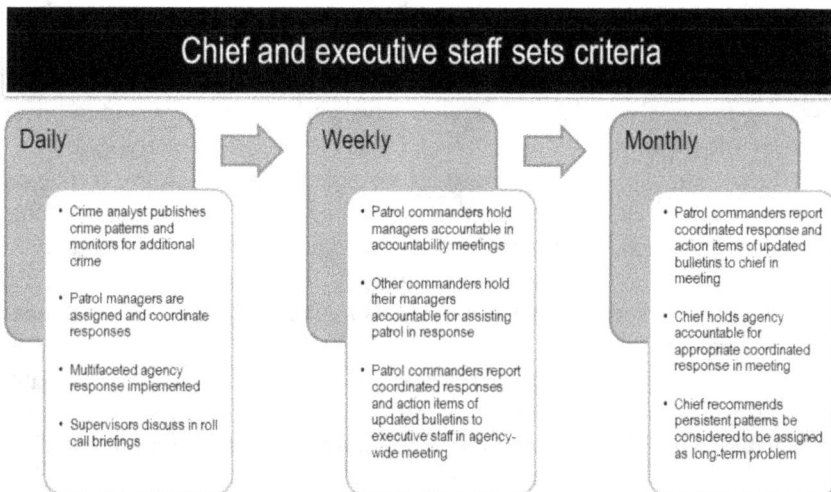

Chief and executive staff sets criteria

Daily
- Crime analyst publishes crime patterns and monitors for additional crime
- Patrol managers are assigned and coordinate responses
- Multifaceted agency response implemented
- Supervisors discuss in roll call briefings

Weekly
- Patrol commanders hold managers accountable in accountability meetings
- Other commanders hold their managers accountable for assisting patrol in response
- Patrol commanders report coordinated responses and action items of updated bulletins to executive staff in agency-wide meeting

Monthly
- Patrol commanders report coordinated response and action items of updated bulletins to chief in meeting
- Chief holds agency accountable for appropriate coordinated response in meeting
- Chief recommends persistent patterns be considered to be assigned as long-term problem

Figure 8.2.   Crime Pattern Process Overview.

PRACTICE-BASED RESEARCH: EFFECTIVENESS OF RESPONSE TO MICRO-TIME HOT SPOTS

Research we enjoy doing is practice-based, which is essentially testing evidence-based strategies implemented in the "real-world" of policing. These strategies are proactive and institutionalized as part of normal operations. Our goal conducting this type of research is to help inform which evidence-based crime reduction strategies are realistic for police to implement and how they can be successfully maintained over time. As an illustration of this type of research, we summarize two studies here—a quasi-experiment and a partially-blocked random controlled trial we conducted with the Port St. Lucie, Florida, Police Department to test the impacts of crime pattern response.[11]

The first study was an ex post facto quasi-experiment that examined 5 years of crime pattern responses to micro-time hot spots of burglary and theft from vehicle occurring in residential areas. During those 5 years, the agency did not respond to every micro-time hot spot, which provided the opportunity to conduct the quasi-experiment. A sophisticated method for matching treatment and comparison cases (i.e., propensity score matching) was used for each crime type separately.

Results for theft from vehicle showed that when police responded with about seven responses per day and for between 2 and 3 weeks, there was nearly a 20 percent reduction in theft from vehicle crime. Also, the micro-time hot spots with response did not last as many days as those with no response. Results for burglary showed six responses per day for between 2 and 3 weeks resulted in over a 20 percent reduction. These micro-time hot spots with police response were resolved in more than half the time than those without a response. In both analyses, responses did not cause crimes to move outside the micro-time hot spot areas. A separate analysis of the effect of response dosage showed more directed patrols per day were related to lower levels of subsequent crime in the crime patterns for both crime types.

In the second study, we replicated the quasi-experimental test of responses to residential burglary and residential theft from vehicle micro-time hot spots using the most rigorous methodology that we could. We conducted a random controlled trial (i.e., experiment). The study was blinded, so no one knew it was being conducted except the chief, two assistant chiefs, two crime analysts, and us.

As was the agency's practice, officers conducted directed patrol as many times as possible during their uncommitted time for a minimum of 14 days. They would spend 15 to 20 minutes at a time actively patrolling (not parked) and, when possible, make suspicious person and vehicle stops, write field interview cards, make traffic stops, give out crime opportunity cards, contact citizens and/or offenders, and make arrests. Over the 2-year experimental period, the department responded to over 100 micro-time hot spots with an average of around five 20-minute responses (1 hour, 40 minutes) per day for 19 days.

Analysis of cumulative time periods—15, 30, 60, and 90 days after the bulletin was published—showed significant differences between the treatment and control groups of micro-time hot spots. At 15 days, the micro-time hot spots receiving response had 79 percent fewer crimes; at 30 days, 74 percent fewer crimes; and at 60 days, 58 percent fewer crimes. Overall, the impact of response after 90 days was a 49 percent reduction. The responses did not cause crimes to move outside the micro-time hot spot areas. The largest effects were seen in the time periods in which micro-time hot spots received response during all or most of the time period. Importantly, the results showed a lasting effect in that the reductions held for 2 months after responses ended. In addition, the department saw significant increases in clearance rates of these two crime types.

Finally, the practical implication of these studies is that the actual crime counts are very low for each micro-time hot spot, so responding to them haphazardly is not likely to have an impact on overall crime. However, a department that institutionalizes the processes into its day-to-day operations can produce substantial reductions and higher clearance rates for targeted crimes.

NOTES

1. Bichler, G., and Gaines, L. (2005). An examination of police officers' insights into problem identification and problem solving. *Crime and Delinquency, 51*(1), 53–74.

McLaughlin, L., Johnson, S. D., Bowers, K. J., Birks, D. J., and Pease, K. (2006). Police perceptions of the long- and short-term spatial distribution of residential burglary. *International Journal of Police Science and Management, 9*(2), 99–111.

Ratcliffe, J. H., and McCullagh, M. (2001). Chasing ghosts? Police perception of high crime areas. *British Journal of Criminology, 41,* 330–41.

Santos, R. B., and Santos, R. G. (2020). Proactive police response in property crime micro-time hot spots: Results from a partially-blocked blind random control trial. *Journal of Quantitative Criminology,* 1–21. DOI 10.1007/s10940-020-09456-8.

2. Science, M., Johnstone, J., Roth, D. E., Guyatt, G., Loeb, M. (2012). Zinc for the treatment of the common cold: A systematic review and meta-analysis of randomized controlled trials. *Canadian Medical Journal, 184*(10), 551–61.

3. Santos, R. B., and Santos, R. G. (2015). Examination of police dosage in residential burglary and theft from vehicle micro-time hot spots. *Crime Science, 4*(27), 1–12.

Santos, R. G., and Santos, R. B. (2015). An ex post facto evaluation of tactical police response in residential theft from vehicle micro-time hot spots. *Journal of Quantitative Criminology, 31*(4), 679–98.

Santos, R. G., and Santos, R. B. (2015). Practice-based research: Ex post facto evaluation of evidence-based police practices implemented in residential burglary micro-time hot spots. *Evaluation Review, 39*(5), 451–79.

Santos and Santos. Proactive police response in property crime micro-time hot spots.

4. Bernasco, W. (2010). A sentimental journey to crime: Effects of residential history on crime location choice. *Criminology, 48*(2), 389–416.

Coupe, T., and Blake, L. (2006). Daylight and darkness targeting strategies and the risks of being seen at residential burglaries. *Criminology, 44,* 431–64.

Johnson, S. D., Lab, S., and Bowers, K. J. (2008). Stable and fluid hot spots of crime: Differentiation and identification. *Built Environment, 34*(1), 32–46.

5. Santos, R. B. (2017). *Crime analysis with crime mapping.* Thousand Oaks, CA: Sage.

6. For a complete list of all pattern types, definitions, and examples, see Santos, *Crime analysis with crime mapping.*

7. Santos and Santos. Examination of police dosage.

Santos and Santos. Proactive police response in property crime micro-time hot spots.

Santos and Santos. An ex post facto evaluation of tactical police response.

Santos and Santos. Practice-based research: Ex post facto evaluation.

8. Johnson, S. D., Summers, L., and Pease, K. (2007). *Vehicle crime: Communicating spatial and temporal patterns.* London: Jill Dando Institute of Crime Science.

9. Braga, A. A., Turchan, B., Papachristos, A. V., and Hureau, D. M. (2019). Hot spots policing of small geographic areas effects on crime. *Campbell Systematic Reviews.* DOI: 10.1002/cl2.1046.

Santos and Santos. Examination of police dosage.

Santos and Santos. Proactive police response in property crime micro-time hot spots.

Santos and Santos. An ex post facto evaluation of tactical police response.

Santos and Santos. Practice-based research: Ex post facto evaluation.

Sherman, L. W. (1990). Police crackdowns: Initial and residual deterrence. *Crime and Justice, 12,* 1–48.

Weisburd, D., and Majmundar, M. K. (Eds.) (2018). *Proactive policing: Effects on crime and communities.* Washington, DC: The National Academies Press.

10. Lum, C., Koper, C. S., Wu, X., Johnson, W., and Stoltz, M. (2020). Examining the empirical realities of proactive policing through systematic observations and computer-aided dispatch data. *Police Quarterly,* 1–28. DOI: 10.1177/1098611119896081.

Koper, C. S. (1995). Just enough police presence: Reducing crime and disorderly behavior by optimizing patrol time in crime hot spots. *Justice Quarterly, 12,* 649–72.

Santos and Santos. Examination of police dosage.

Santos and Santos. Proactive police response in property crime micro-time hot spots.

11. Santos and Santos. Examination of police dosage.

Santos and Santos. An ex post facto evaluation of tactical police response.

Santos and Santos. Practice-based research.

Santos and Santos. Proactive police response in property crime micro-time hot spots.

Chapter Nine

Long-Term Crime Reduction: Problem Offenders, Problem Locations, and Problem Areas

Long-term problems are the most complex crime and disorder problems addressed in Stratified Policing. They are sets of related activity occurring over many months, seasons, or years that stem from systematic opportunities created by everyday behavior and environment. They can consist of common disorder activity, quality-of-life issues, and serious criminal activity. Long-term problems are offenders, locations, and defined areas within a jurisdiction that are most concerning for the community and the police. The level of analysis and development of responses for long-term problems are much more involved than for immediate and short-term problems.

As discussed previously, Stratified Policing incorporates place-based, person-focused, problem solving, and community-based approaches. Because long-term problems have manifested over longer periods of time and have become complex. Strategies derived from these approaches have to be applied much more extensively, which requires higher levels of internal and external collaboration and implementation over a longer period of time. While involvement of the community is important for each problem level, long-term problems will require development of broader, more comprehensive community engagement and partnership strategies.

The problem-solving process (SARA) is the basis for addressing each type of problem. For short-term problems, analysis and assessment are straightforward and the responses are implemented in the short term. For long-term problems, the entire problem solving process is more comprehensive because it matches the complexity of problem addressed. Crime analysis involves more than police data, and responses require various partners as well as take more time to implement and resolve the problem.

For long-term problems, the problem analysis triangle is central for better understanding the underlying opportunities and causes of each chronic problem. Responses are tailored based on the examination of the offender, place, victim, and targets with the objective of preventing crime or disorder activity by deterring and reducing opportunities. Developed from the environmental criminology theories, situational crime prevention responses are implemented often in collaboration with external partners.[1] That is, responses address underlying causes of the problem, so in most cases traditional police activities, such as directed patrol and arrest, have to be supplemented with more in-depth responses that engage citizens, business owners, community groups, and other nonpolice entities.

While long-term problems are manifested differently in individual communities, police face many of the same types of problems. Examples include gun violence by young offenders, street robbery, burglary of single-family homes, and disorder at budget motels. Research on the effectiveness of the problem-solving approach is based mostly on practical evaluations of police problem-solving efforts. The evidence suggests that the approach has strong effects on crime and can have positive effects on the community.[2]

Consequently, this chapter covers the processes for addressing three types of long-term problems, called problem offenders, problem locations, and problem areas. Although these are distinct types, they share commonalities in how they are addressed within Stratified Policing, particularly in accountability. Thus, we provide a discussion of identification and analysis, response, and assessment for each problem type separately. Then we cover the accountability mechanisms for them all collectively.

PROBLEM OFFENDERS

The first type of long-term problem is a problem offender. These are individuals who are a concern to both the community and the police because they are chronic repeat offenders. They commit a disproportionate amount of crime and are problematic within the community. The goal is to identify these individuals and develop long-term solutions to reduce or stop them from reoffending. Problem offenders are defined as follows:

> Individual people who have been arrested for and/or convicted of a disproportionate amount of crime incidents usually over more than a year. Problem offenders are typically specific individuals who live in the jurisdiction. However, they may also be individuals who live outside the jurisdiction but are responsible for notable amounts of crime at problem locations or in problem areas.

Problem offenders move through different settings and systematically take advantage of different victims and places. The concept of the 80/20 rule applies to problem offenders, in that a small number of offenders commit a large percentage of the crimes. This fact helps police understand that selecting the most chronic offenders who contribute to a disproportionate amount of crime or disorder can have the most return on a police agency's proactive efforts. In addition, research and practice have shown most offenders commit crimes near where they live, work, and frequent.[3] Therefore, focusing on specific problem offenders living in high-crime areas should be emphasized as part of any person-focused strategy.

There are obviously problem offenders who come from outside a jurisdiction to commit their crimes. Implementing proactive person-focused responses for these problem offenders is more difficult since responses will involve other jurisdictions. The main focus is in high-crime areas that have problem offenders living or frequenting the area on a regular basis. To make person-focused responses realistic to the agency's daily operations, the primary focus is on problem offenders who contribute to crime or disorder at problem locations or in problem areas that have been assigned.

We cannot stress enough the importance of any person-focused response being carried out in a manner that conveys its purpose to the community. The community should be aware that the police are focusing their efforts on specific individuals and why. Also, the community should understand that the police are not doing random and/or general sweeps in their neighborhoods. The police should communicate with the community that these are specific chronic problem offenders, so they are worthy of extra attention by the police. This is important because the person-focused responses should be seen as legitimate by the community. In addition, the responses may include different types of partnerships with citizens, community groups, and other criminal justice entities and social services.

Assigned Responsibility: Investigations Manager

The investigations manager (e.g., lieutenant) is assigned problem offenders and is responsible to ensure person-focused responses are carried out. These responses are within the scope of responsibility and skills of what detectives already do. They are specifically trained in interviewing techniques and have the type of schedule that allows them to contact individuals at different times. In addition, most repeat offender programs are typically housed in the criminal investigations division.

There are several reasons investigations managers are assigned responsibility. Problem offenders are more demanding to address than the known offenders who are contacted in crime patterns. They also require more internal and external coordination of resources than those involved in significant incidents. Thus, the problem offender process engages all the ranks within investigations. The investigations managers, by the rank they hold, already have the necessary amount of authority and autonomy to make decisions, hold investigations personnel accountable, influence external partners, and coordinate resources. Therefore, investigations managers are held accountable for problem offenders to cultivate and maintain the necessary partnerships and ensure the required responses are occurring.

Identification and Analysis of Problem Offenders

There are a range of crime analysis techniques that are used to identify problem offenders. We recommend crime analysts keep the technique simple. The selection of data and how the offenders are prioritized should be done in a thoughtful and meaningful way and guided by the agency's crime reduction goals and community concerns. The number of problem offenders identified and assigned should be manageable since tailored, and sometimes in-depth, responses take place. Importantly, we do not recommend using off-the-shelf repeat offender identification software or algorithms unless crime analysts can specifically control all the analysis parameters to ensure offenders are selected in a judicious way.

The identification of problem offenders results in a prioritized list of individuals. We recommend examining at least twelve months of arrest data that coincides with one or more crime reduction goals. There are a variety of ways to prioritize offenders. A straightforward technique that can be used and easily duplicated when additional offenders need to be identified is a descending frequency of arrests by offender with percent of the total. Another is an 80/20 analysis.[4]

To consider seriousness in addition to frequency, each crime type can be weighted. For example, violent crimes might be multiplied by 2, so an offender arrested for 3 robberies (value of 6) is higher than an offender committing 5 theft from vehicles (value of 5). We strongly caution against the use of drug arrests and minor criminal activity when deciding on a point system because the purpose is to prioritize problem offenders based on predatory crimes. Regardless of the technique, the chief and executive staff decide on the data parameters for identification and approve the method used by the crime analyst for prioritization.

Depending on the agency's crime reduction goals and geographic deployment of the investigations division, one problem offender list might be created for the entire jurisdiction or multiple lists by geographic area. In addition, we recommend a separate list be created for problem areas, which allows the agency to double down on its focus in particular problem areas that have been assigned to a patrol commander.

Once assigned, a standardized packet of analysis is automatically provided by crime analysts to investigations managers for each problem offender. Because the focus is a person and not a location or area, the type of information follows what is typically called an offender "work up." The purpose of the analysis is to provide the managers the necessary information to develop responses tailored to that individual. The packet is a comprehensive report containing a complete criminal history from the national crime database, corrections history and current probation/parole status, gang affiliation, and any other contacts made with the police agency, including as a victim, a witness, in calls for service, and traffic citations. Associates, family members, residence history, history with city services, and social media activity are also included. As part of the analysis process, while the responses are being implemented, crime analysts monitor each offender and provide updates to this information as needed.

Response to Problem Offenders

Person-focused responses are not about the police being either "tough" or "soft" on problem offenders. Responses should be specific and appropriate based on the particular problem offender. There are different approaches that can be used because not all offenders are the same or offend for the same reasons. As with every police strategy we recommend, the problem-solving process is used to address problem offenders. Research shows person-focused proactive strategies have an impact on both offender recidivism and crime in the jurisdiction, so the goal is to identify these chronic offenders and tailor the responses to their situations.[5]

The primary objective of person-focused responses is to prevent crime by deterring specific and known high-rate offenders.[6] The central responses are focused on direct interaction with offenders and communication of clear incentives for compliance and consequences for criminal activity.[7] Police often confront offenders to explicitly outline what will happen if they continue committing crime. Some responses include organized face-to-face meetings with offenders along with family, community members, and others to reinforce the seriousness of the process and compliance. In many cases, these responses are used for offenders vulnerable to criminal justice sanctions. Once the agency begins systematically addressing problem offenders, there should be an emphasis on developing long-term partnerships with federal and state prosecutors as well as correctional agencies to include probation. This is done so certain responses are more streamlined and effective through communication and collaboration about specific problem offenders.

Person-focused responses may be different based on whether the agency's focus is on serious violent crime versus property crime or on adults versus juveniles. Equally important is incorporating other non-criminal-justice external partners that can provide solutions that are nonpunitive. Depending on the circumstance, a preventive component should be incorporated into responses by providing opportunities and services that can help certain problem offenders from reoffending (i.e., outreach efforts).

As noted earlier, person-focused responses should be carried out where the community understands that police are focused on particular offenders for good reason and are not selecting them without purpose or conducting general sweeps of neighborhoods. The police need to communicate to the community that they are focused on specific chronic problem offenders committing serious crime in their neighborhoods. Thus, they are worthy of extra attention by the police. The combination of punitive, supportive, outreach, and communication with the community provides a multitude of person-focused, evidence-based responses that the investigations section can select from to effectively address problem offenders.

To help in the process of developing and choosing responses, investigations managers should also consult the problem and response guidebooks that have been developed for police problem-solving efforts.[8] Some guides that are specifically relevant for problem offenders include the following:

- Focused Deterrence of High-Risk Offenders
- Analyzing and Responding to Repeat Offending
- Monitoring Offenders on Conditional Release
- Retaliatory Violent Disputes
- Gun Violence among Serious Young Offenders
- Drive-by Shootings

Assessment

The evaluation of whether responses to problem offenders are working is a straightforward approach with two types of assessment. The first type is whether problem offenders are deterred from committing crimes. To assess this, crime analysts keep track of each problem offender's arrests no matter the type of crime or where the crime/arrest occurred. In other words, they consider all the problem offender's criminal activity known to the criminal justice system. The agency considers the lack of crime for a certain time period along with other life circumstances to determine when their efforts are successful.

The second type is if the problem offender is arrested, there is a successful prosecution. That is, when a problem offender is arrested the investigations manager ensures that there is collaboration with other criminal justice agencies to achieve a successful conclusion. How these two types of assessments are used to prioritize problem offenders for discussion in accountability meetings is provided at the end of this chapter in the accountability section.

Practice-Based Research: Effectiveness of Person-Focused Response in Problem Areas

There is a lot of good research on person-focused crime reduction strategies. We thought it would be relevant here to discuss an example of practice-based research we have done on this topic.[9] Through a federal grant, we had the opportunity to test a prevention-oriented, person-focused response in property crime problem areas. The research was based on the premise that offenders commit crime near where they live, so if police deter and/or prevent problem offenders living in problem areas from committing additional crimes, they can reduce the overall crime in a particular problem area.

The goal of the responses was to influence the offenders' perceptions of their risk of being caught committing crimes near where they lived by strengthening formal surveillance and reducing anonymity of the offenders. Since the focus was nonviolent property crimes and the majority of offenders were juveniles and young adults, the responses were primarily prevention and deterrence oriented. Instead of the responses seeking apprehension or enhanced prosecution, they involved direct communication with offenders and their families about stopping criminal activity and improving their life circumstances.

Property crime problem areas were defined exclusively as residential areas. Forty-eight areas were identified, and twenty-four were assigned as treatment and control problem areas as part of an experimental design. Interactions with each offender and/or family member were meant to build rapport between them and the detectives who made the contacts. Through this interaction, offenders understood the detectives could recognize them, their family, and associates and knew where they lived. They were also aware that the detectives would be driving in their neighborhoods and may visit their homes at unpredictable times. Because the majority of offenders were juveniles or young adults living with their parent(s) and sibling(s), the detectives interacted with family members as well to encourage them to urge the offenders to change their patterns of behavior.

The detectives conducted curfew checks on the offenders with correctional sanctions, which was the primary mechanism for regular and legitimate contact with an offender. When there were curfew violations, the detectives spoke to the offenders and/or family members to reinforce the importance of following their probation and doing the right thing. The detectives typically did not arrest for the violations or call the probation officers unless it was necessary to reinforce the importance of following their sanctions.

The impact on crime and recidivism of the problem offenders was promising. The findings indicated that the treatment areas declined in property crime 21 percent relative to the control areas. Problem offenders were arrested significantly less during the response with a 68 percent reduction from the 9 months before the response started. As part of the evaluation, we also conducted interviews with thirty-four offenders and twenty-nine family members. This was done after the responses were over to explore whether the contact with police detectives had negative consequences.[10]

There were consistent themes in both the offenders and their family members' responses. They were positive about their interactions with the detectives. They also agreed the detectives influenced the offenders to commit less crime and to stop associating with people who might get them into "trouble." Offenders with sanctions and their family members also agreed the detectives influenced them to follow the terms of probation more closely than they did before the program. Parents expressed that their relationships improved because the offenders listened to them more and spent more time at home than before the detectives' contacts.

PROBLEM LOCATIONS

The second type of long-term problem is a problem location. The goal is to identify the most problematic locations and develop long-term solutions that reduce or prevent crime, disorder, and quality-of-life issues. A problem location is defined as follows:

> Individual address or distinct location with multiple addresses where there is a concentration of crime, disorder, and/or quality of life activity usually over more than a year. They are typically managed by a single entity. The nature and purpose of the location as well as the behavior of various victims and offenders in and immediately surrounding the location manifests the problem.

Problem locations can be one distinct business or building, such as a bar, convenience store, group home, or large retail box store. Or they can be distinct entities that are larger in geography and have multiple addresses, such as an apartment complex, a mobile home park, or a retail business plaza.

The concept of the 80/20 rule (i.e., a small number of places are responsible for a large amount of the problem) helps understand that addressing locations that contribute to a disproportionate amount of crime or disorder can have a large return from an agency's crime reduction efforts. In addition, problem locations are manifestations of consistent repeat incidents that have reached a point where they are no longer considered short term. The goal is to understand the underlying opportunities and develop tailored long-term solutions that are implemented by police in collaboration with external entities and the community.

Assigned Responsibility: Patrol Managers

Problem locations are assigned to patrol managers (e.g., lieutenants). If geographically deployed, patrol managers are assigned problem locations in their assigned areas. If not, they are assigned locations based on the time and nature of the issue or based on an equal workload. Patrol shift managers, including those working midnight shift, should be assigned problem locations because responses can be carried out various times of the day, evening, and overnight. Although patrol managers utilize the appropriate resources from throughout the organization, they are responsible to actively lead the effort. Their responsibilities should not be delegated.

Patrol managers are assigned responsibility for similar reasons as crime patterns. Problem locations are more complex and require more coordination and resources than lower-level problems. Their responses require a higher level of cooperation and collaboration with the location's manager/owner and the community to address the underlying issues. Stratified Policing seeks to engage different ranks, and patrol managers are better positioned within the patrol division to set aside the time it takes to address problem locations. Also, by their rank and job responsibilities, patrol managers have the necessary authority and autonomy within the organization to make decisions and coordinate resources across shifts and divisions.

Identification and Analysis of Problem Locations

There are two separate ways problem locations are identified. The first is through the repeat incident process discussed earlier. This is when repeat incident locations (assigned to patrol supervisors) that are not resolved are moved up to the problem location level and assigned to patrol managers. Crime analysts assess repeat incidents continually and initiate this change based on agency criteria. The second way is through systematic analysis initiated by crime analysts.

To identify problem locations, crime analysts usually use 12 months of data for goal crimes, disorder, and/or quality of life issues. The locations can be identified within individual geographic areas (e.g., districts) or for the entire jurisdiction. It is important that the number of problem locations that are assigned to each patrol manager ensures realistic expectations for the managers' workload. Which locations and how many are decided by the chief based on resources, agency-wide crime reduction efforts, community concerns, and the nature of the problem location.

Problem locations are more complex than short-term problems. So, once they are assigned, a packet of analysis examining at least twelve months of data is automatically produced by crime analysts for each problem location. The packet is used by the patrol manager to understand the long-term under-lying issues and develop responses. It is necessary for crime analysts to dig deeper into the data based on what they find in order to provide meaningful results. We recommend this analysis cover some or all of the following:

- Citizen-generated calls for service: Analysis of all calls by type, time of day/day of week, address, disposition
- Repeat incidents: Information about the issues and responses that have oc-curred if the address ever came up as a repeat incident location
- Officer-generated calls for service: Analysis of all calls by type, time of day/day of week, address, disposition, amount of officer time spent
- Crime reports: Analysis of all crime reports by type, date of occurrence, time of day/day of week, address, disposition; crime patterns identified and responded to
- Arrest data: Analysis of all arrests by name, charge, date of arrest, address of arrest
- Known offenders: Offenders with high levels of arrest related to the crimes that are occurring at the problem location
- Surrounding area: Analysis of the area immediately around the problem lo-cation might also be conducted to help better understand why the problem location is an issue
- Non-police information: Owner, renter, occupants, zoning, taxes, code violations, and property history of the location

Response to Problem Locations

Patrol managers use the problem analysis triangle and the crime analysis packet, as well as other information on potential effective responses, to de-velop a long-term plan for addressing the problem location. Managers are responsible to initiate the response plan, coordinate with other internal and external partners, and utilize the agency's resources, as appropriate. The patrol division, as well as other units and divisions in the organization, car-ries out the specific responses. The patrol managers actively assist with the responses and are ultimately responsible to ensure they are coordinated and implemented correctly.

Generally, problem locations require similar police responses that were discussed for short-term problems, such as directed patrol, offender contacts, and proactive arrests. However, the patrol managers must think deeper about the very specific nature of the problem location and what else is necessary. As a result, they will develop more comprehensive responses to directly address the underlying issues causing the chronic problem. For example, responses may also include utilizing other city resources that are not directly controlled by the police as well as developing partnerships with the community and business/homeowners.

The response plan is developed based on understanding how opportunities are created and acted upon as well as understanding how the location or type of place compares to similar, non-problematic places. For example, understanding why one apartment complex is experiencing significantly more crime and disorder than other similar complexes nearby can help the patrol manager think about the cause of the problem. Overwhelmingly, research shows problem-solving in chronic locations is effective in reducing crime, disorder, and quality-of-life issues.[11] To help in the process of developing and choosing responses, patrol managers should also consult problem and response guidebooks that have been developed for police problem solving efforts.[12] Some examples of the problem, response, and tool guides that support responses to problem locations are the following:

- Shoplifting
- Assaults in and around Bars
- Disorder at Budget Motels
- Drug Dealing in Privately Owned Apartment Complexes
- Theft of Customers' Personal Property in Cafés and Bars
- Robbery of Convenience Stores
- Robbery of Pharmacies
- Understanding Risky Facilities
- Partnering with Businesses to Address Public Safety Problems
- Using CPTED in Problem Solving
- Using Civil Actions against Property to Control Crime Problems
- Video Surveillance of Public Places

Assessment

The assessment process to determine success for problem location responses is straightforward. Each month, problem locations are formally presented by patrol commanders to determine if the responses are effective. Since problem locations usually require responses over several months, crime analysts provide the commander one evaluation product per month with statistics for each problem location. This allows for a quick assessment to determine whether responses are working.

The problem location evaluation product should be standardized and have the same format and general content. However, the analysis is specific to each problem location based on the issues addressed. For example, if the problem location was assigned because of the large number of assaults, drug sales, and disorderly conduct, the product would illustrate those three crimes. Depending on the data, crime analysts may break up the different types of crimes and create multiple charts, or include them in one.

Either way, the results should be meaningful and straightforward in order to evaluate the impact of the responses at the problem location. To do this, the analysis should compare activity levels before and after the problem location was assigned and responses start. After the first month, crime analysts simply update the chart each month using the same data, which assists in the ongoing assessment. This analysis is done until the problem location is resolved. For an example of the crime analysis evaluation product we recommend for the patrol commanders' monthly presentations, see chapter 10.

Importantly, it is rare that a problem location is completely resolved where there are no additional calls for service or crimes. Thus, deciding when a problem location is satisfactorily resolved is a judgment call by the chief. The chief's decision can be based on several factors including achieving a certain reduction in crime, how the numbers relate to the crime reduction goals, and/or if it is realistically possible to reduce the problem any further. The main point is to reduce the problem location to an acceptable and manageable level (i.e., a new normal).

PROBLEM AREAS

The final type of long-term problem is a problem area, which is the most complex problem. Problem areas are also called "hot spots" by police. Because Stratified Policing addresses micro-time hot spots, the term "problem area" is used to avoid confusion. Problem areas are defined as follows:

> Relatively small, defined areas that have disproportionately more criminal and/or disorder activity than other areas within a jurisdiction. Problem areas are stable and persist over a long period of time—more than a year. Problem areas contain significant incidents, crime patterns, repeat incidents, problem offenders, and problem locations.

Problem areas are identified by crime analysts as groups of streets and/or areas within neighborhoods or commercial corridors. They are usually the most concerning problems to the community and the police because they have the most crime and disorder issues within a jurisdiction. Generally, by the time they are identified, the area has been experiencing a consistent high level of crimes and has been notably worse than other areas in the community for a long time.

We know from the "law of crime concentration"[13] that crime does cluster by place, and the clusters are specific, stable, and predictable over time. Research and practice have definitively confirmed it is worthwhile for police to focus on problem areas in order to reduce crime. Importantly, research has shown police responding to these areas does not displace crime to other areas, but instead reduces crime.[14]

As long-term problems, problem areas contain immediate and short-term problems (i.e., significant incidents, repeat incidents, and crime patterns) as well as other long-term problems (i.e., problem offenders and problem locations). This is why they are concerning to the community, the most complex to understand, and the most difficult to remedy. This is also why identifying and responding to problem areas must include both short-term and long-term responses that match the temporal nature of crime and disorder problems that consistently occur in these defined areas. Although all problems incorporate responses derived from place-based, problem-solving, person-focused, and community-based approaches, problem areas require the most thought, effort, and coordination of strategies and resources.

Assigned Responsibility: Patrol Commanders

When an agency is geographically deployed, problem areas are assigned to patrol geographic area commanders (e.g., district captains). Although patrol commanders use a range of the agency's resources, they are responsible to design a response plan and actively lead the effort. Their responsibilities should not be delegated. Patrol commanders are assigned problem areas because they are the most complex to solve and they require the highest level of cooperation and collaboration within the police organization as well as with external criminal justice and community partners. Patrol commanders are better positioned to set aside the time needed to engage different ranks and areas in the agency and to work with others at the commander level. Finally, by the rank they already hold, they have the necessary amount of authority and autonomy to make decisions and coordinate resources necessary to properly resolve problem areas.

Identification and Analysis of Problem Areas

To proactively and systematically identify problem areas, crime analysts use 12 to 36 months of data selected based on goal crimes and community concerns. Data from a combination of goals and concerns should be used. We recommend crime analysts start by identifying two to three problem areas per geographic area (e.g., district). This provides the chief the opportunity to select what is to be assigned based on what is realistic and best suits the agency's goals and community concerns.

In this context, crime analysts do not identify problem areas for the patrol commanders, but for the chief. The patrol commanders do not have a choice in what is assigned to them. This is similar to how patrol officers do not choose which calls for service they respond to; patrol supervisors do not choose repeat incidents; and patrol managers do not choose crime patterns. This process is transparent and is completely based on the goals, community concerns, crime levels, and the chief's discretion.

To identify problem areas, we recommend a straightforward method. Importantly, the result of identification is a set of specifically defined areas. These areas are distinct with concrete borders drawn on a map. This is essential for response and accountability processes. That is, once defined, patrol commanders are responsible for implementing responses within that designated area. They are evaluated based on the activity occurring within those static boundaries.

Crime analysts begin identification by creating a density map for a specific geographic area of focus (e.g., entire jurisdiction or one district), and then they select areas with the highest density. Figure 9.1 shows an initial density map with several high-density areas—the highest in the middle of the map with the darkest color. Next, crime analysts create individual maps for each selected area showing the crime/disorder incidents to see where the crimes occurred within the areas.

Considering the locations of the incidents and how they are concentrated, crime analysts determine the exact borders of the problem area. It is helpful to use satellite images to see buildings, streets, and open spaces. The decisions about borders are made based on where the crimes occur in the area as well as subjective assessment of the street network, the area characteristics, and the realistic size for directed patrol and long-term responses. Figure 9.2 is an example of a map with the defined borders of a problem area.

Once problem areas are identified and assigned by the chief to the patrol commander(s), crime analysts automatically conduct more in-depth analysis on the problem area and provide a packet of analysis based on 12 to 36 months of data. The packet is used by the patrol commander to help understand the long-term underlying issues and develop responses. It is necessary

Figure 9.1. Example of an Initial Density Map
Map was created using ArcGIS® software by Esri. ArcGIS® and ArcMap™ are the intellectual property of Esri and are used herein under license. Copyright © Esri. All rights reserved. For more information about Esri® software, please visit www.esri.com.

Figure 9.2. Final Problem Area Example
Map. Google. (n.d.). Satellite Map. Retrieved February 7, 2020 from URL www.google.com/maps.

for crime analysts to dig deeper into the data based on what they find in order to provide meaningful results. We recommend the analysis cover some or all of the following:

- Citizen-generated calls for service: analysis of all calls by type, time of day/day of week, address, disposition
- Officer-generated calls for service: analysis of all calls by type, time of day/day of week, address, disposition, amount of officer time spent
- Crime reports: analysis of all crime reports by type, date of occurrence, time of day/day of week, address, disposition
- Arrest data: analysis of all arrests occurring in the problem area by name, charge, date of arrest, address of arrest
- Known offenders: analysis of offenders living in the problem area meeting the agency's criteria of being a problem offender and/or offenders with high levels of arrest related to the crimes that are mainly contributing to the problem area
- Repeat incidents, crime patterns, and problem locations: an overview of these problems that have occurred in the problem area for the last year
- Non-police information: locations of churches, schools, businesses; existing neighborhood groups; official city information (e.g., zoning, licenses, code enforcement violations, taxes); other relevant information

Response to Problem Areas

The goal of the problem-solving process is to understand the underlying behaviors and opportunities occurring in the problem area and develop long-term solutions implemented by police in collaboration with the community and external entities. To be most effective, it is necessary to incorporate responses derived from place-based, problem-solving, person-focused, and community-based approaches. Although all of these strategies are infused throughout Stratified Policing, a problem area response plan requires a higher level of coordination and in-depth problem solving to identify the most appropriate responses from each approach.

We recommend, as part of the overall responses to problem areas, for crime analysts to proactively conduct and prioritize analysis of problem offenders, problem locations, crime patterns, and repeat incidents within problem areas. This allows patrol commanders to focus the agency's efforts and make an even more concentrated impact. By doing so, they can direct resources in a multifaceted and coordinated way into the problem area.

Essentially, all the strategies discussed in this book for short- and long-term problems are used in problem areas. Patrol commanders take the lead on their individual problem areas, and other commanders throughout the organization support their efforts. These problem areas require a lot of effort to implement and sustain the selected responses. While it is important for all processes in Stratified Policing, especially for problem areas, everyone must play their part and do their job so that smaller amounts contributed from each section of the organization result in a comprehensive, coordinated approach.

There are a variety of possible responses to problem areas that can be implemented, but they are highly dependent on the type of activity, the police and community resources, and the local environment. The main point here is that, when developing their response plans, patrol commanders think beyond deploying only police resources to reduce crime because those resources can only go so far in having long-term impact. The commanders must include an emphasis on collaboration with community, businesses, and other criminal justice entities in their plans. They must also actively participate in community engagement, foster relationships, and facilitate collaboration themselves.

As noted throughout the book, great care should be taken to communicate and engage citizens before and as the responses are carried out. Effort should be made so the community understands the purpose of police responses in the area. They should be aware that there are clear reasons (e.g., high crime numbers reported by the citizens themselves) for the focus in that area versus others in the jurisdiction. An overwhelming majority of the people living in any given problem area are not contributing to the problem, but instead, are part of the solution great care should be taken as police deploy specific strategies in these areas so they are not construed as negative by the community. Emphasis should be placed on actions that enhance police legitimacy and community trust.

Finally, there are examples of effective responses that have been used in different situations and environments for similar types of problems. To help in the process of developing and choosing responses, patrol commanders should also consult problem and response guidebooks that have been developed for police problem-solving efforts.[15] Some examples of problem, response, and tool guides that support responses to problem areas are the following:

- Street Robbery
- Home Invasion Robbery
- Burglary of Single-Family Houses
- Burglary of Retail Establishments
- Thefts of and from Cars on Residential Streets and Driveways
- Drug Dealing in Open-Air Markets
- Disorderly Youth in Public Places
- Chronic Public Inebriation
- Street Prostitution
- Homeless Encampments

- Abandoned Buildings and Lots
- Using Civil Actions against Property to Control Crime Problems
- Improving Street Lighting to Reduce Crime in Residential Areas
- Dealing with Crime and Disorder in Urban Parks
- Crime Prevention Publicity Campaigns
- Shifting and Sharing Responsibility for Public Safety Problems
- Using CPTED in Problem Solving
- Partnering with Businesses to Address Public Safety Problems

Assessment

Density maps are only used in the analysis process to identify problem areas. They are not used for evaluation of the impact on crime and disorder or in accountability meetings. We recommend a straightforward way to evaluate the impact of the responses in problem areas. Most importantly, evaluation measures come from the data used to identify the problem areas, so patrol commanders are held accountable for the activity they have been tasked to address. In addition, success of the responses should be evaluated based on activity occurring within the boundaries of the problem area. Again, this is why it is essential the problem area borders be clearly defined, static, and determined in a meaningful way.

The assessment process for problem areas is similar to the process for problem locations. Each month, problem areas are formally presented by the patrol commander to determine if the responses are effective. Since problem areas usually require responses over several months, crime analysts provide the commander one chart per month with statistics for each problem area, which allows for a quick assessment to determine whether responses are working.

The problem area evaluation chart should be standardized and have the same format and general content. However, each chart should be specific to the problem area. For example, if the problem area was assigned because of the high number of robberies, assaults, and burglaries, the analysis would assess those three crimes. The results should be meaningful and straightforward in order to evaluate the impact of the responses in the problem area. To do this, the analysis should compare activity levels before and after the problem area was assigned and responses start. After the first month, crime analysts simply update the chart each month using the same data, which assists in the ongoing assessment. This analysis is done until the problem area is resolved. For an example of an evaluation product we recommend for the patrol commanders' monthly presentations, see chapter 10.

Importantly, a problem area will not be completely resolved where there are no additional crimes. Assessing when a problem area has been satisfactorily resolved is a judgment call by the chief. The chief's decision can be based on a combination of things. These can include achieving a certain percent or total count reduction, how the numbers relate to the crime reduction goals, community perceptions, and if it is realistically possible to reduce the problem any further. The main point is to reduce the activity in the problem area to an acceptable and manageable level (i.e., a new normal).

LONG-TERM PROBLEMS: ACCOUNTABILITY MEETINGS AND DOCUMENTATION

As the most complex issues police face, long-term problems are automatically and formally presented in the monthly agency-wide meeting. The patrol and investigations commanders are held accountable for progress of responses at the weekly agency-wide meetings. In the monthly agency-wide meetings, they are held accountable by the chief for responses as well as their impact on crime. The following is a breakdown of how the accountability meetings are utilized for problem offenders, problem locations, and problem areas:

- Daily patrol briefings: Since these problems are addressed for many months, there is no need to discuss the larger strategies every day. However, this meeting can be used to communicate responses needed for that day.
- Weekly patrol meetings: When geographically deployed, the patrol area commander (e.g., captain) and managers (e.g., lieutenants) discuss ongoing long-term problems. These meetings do not entail formal presentations but focus on ensuring how well long-term problems are being responded to and confirming that collaboration occurs. This meeting is used for holding supervisors and managers accountable as well as preparing commanders for the weekly agency-wide meeting.
- Weekly agency-wide meetings: Executive staff (e.g., assistant chief) holds patrol and investigations commanders accountable for their respective long-term problems. These meetings allow the executive staff to ensure responses are progressing as planned. Discussions of long-term problems are action-oriented and focus on facilitating coordination among commanders.
- Monthly agency-wide meetings: Patrol commanders make formal presentations on the problem locations and areas. The chief holds them accountable for implementing their response plans and uses monthly evaluation statistics to determine success of their efforts. Support commanders may contribute to the conversation about problem locations and problem areas and are not responsible for reporting out; however, the chief holds them accountable for providing patrol the assistance it needs.

    The investigations commander makes a formal presentation on selected problem offenders. That is, it may not be realistic to have the investigations commander present all the assigned problem offenders each month, so consistent criteria can be developed to prioritize offenders for the commander's presentation. For example, the chief may require the commander to present only on the top five out of a list of ten problem offenders that were assigned. Or the chief may require presentations for only offenders who were arrested or implicated in a crime (i.e., suspect) after responses started in order to hold the commander accountable for the case through prosecution.

To assist supervisors, managers, and commanders, we recommend using an intranet system to document responses to long-term problems. Agencies that have implemented Stratified Policing have found intranet systems are a robust way to track long-term problem responses, especially because there are a lot of moving parts and the responses occur over a long period of time (see chapter 10).

Documentation for long-term problems consists of the electronic formal presentations commanders give at the monthly meetings. These contain the responses that have been implemented and the evaluation statistics. The action items on each presentation and those that come up in the meetings themselves are used by the chief in subsequent months to hold the commanders accountable. When a problem location or area has been resolved, or problem offender has been prosecuted, the final presentation becomes documentation of all the work that was done and can be used as an example for addressing similar problems in the future.

STRATIFIED POLICING
LONG-TERM PROBLEM PROCESS OVERVIEW

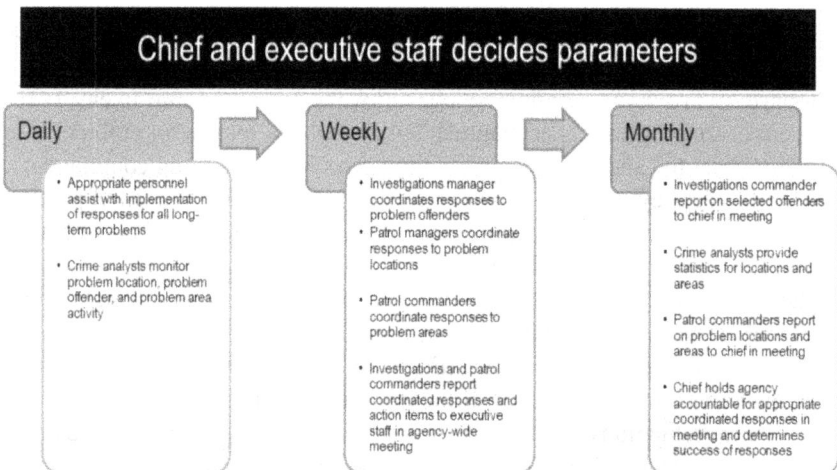

Figure 9.3.   Long-Term Problem Process Overview.

NOTES

1. Clarke, R. V. (1980). Situational crime prevention: Theory and practice. *British Journal of Criminology, 20,* 136–47.

Clarke, R. V. (Ed.) (1997). *Situational crime prevention: Successful case studies* (2nd ed.). New York: Harrow and Heston.

2. Weisburd, D., and Majmundar, M. K. (Eds.) (2018). *Proactive policing: Effects on crime and communities.* Washington, DC: The National Academies Press.

3. Bernasco, W. (2010). A sentimental journey to crime: Effects of residential history on crime location choice. *Criminology, 48*(2), 389–416.

4. For specific techniques, see Santos, R. B. (2017). *Crime analysis with crime mapping.* Thousand Oaks, CA: Sage.

5. Braga, A., and Weisburd, D. (2012). The effects of focused deterrence strategies on crime: A systematic review and meta-analysis of the empirical evidence. *Journal of Research in Crime and Delinquency, 49*(3), 323–58.

6. Weisburd and Majmundar. *Proactive policing.*

7. Weisburd and Majmundar. *Proactive policing*, 58.

8. See Center for Problem-Oriented Policing (https://popcenter.asu.edu/) and the Office of Community-Oriented Policing Resource Center (https://cops.usdoj.gov/ric/ric.php) for copies of these guidebooks.

9. Santos, R. B., and Santos, R. G. (2016). Offender-focused police strategies in residential burglary and theft from vehicle hot spots: A partially blocked randomized controlled trial. *Journal of Experimental Criminology, 12*(3), 373–402.

10. Santos, R. G. (2018). Offender and family member perceptions after an offender-focused hot spots policing strategy. *Policing: An International Journal, 41*(3), 386–400.

11. Weisburd and Majmundar. *Proactive policing.*

12. See Center for Problem-Oriented Policing (https://popcenter.asu.edu/) and the Office of Community-Oriented Policing Resource Center (https://cops.usdoj.gov/ric/ric.php) for copies of these guidebooks.

13. Weisburd, D. (2015). The law of crime concentration and the criminology of place. *Criminology, 53*(2), 133–57.

14. Braga, A. A., Turchan, B., Papachristos, A. V., and Hureau, D. M. (2019). Hot spots policing of small geographic areas effects on crime. *Campbell Systematic Reviews.* DOI: 10.1002/cl2.1046.

15. See Center for Problem-Oriented Policing (https://popcenter.asu.edu/) and the Office of Community-Oriented Policing Resource Center (https://cops.usdoj.gov/ric/ric.php) for copies of these guidebooks.

Chapter Ten

Accountability and Meeting Structure

One of the most important elements of successful Stratified Policing implementation is having an engaged chief who has a supportive executive staff. As with anything in police organizations, leadership plays a crucial role in setting the tone for accountability, and it must come from the highest ranks. However, to fully institutionalize proactive crime reduction, leaders must establish mechanisms of accountability that are strong enough to overcome cultural resistance and influence formal (e.g., supervisor to officer) and informal (i.e., peer-to-peer) accountability.

Police leaders should be out in front actively demonstrating what is most valuable to the agency. When implementing proactive crime reduction, police leaders need to cultivate the organizational environment and become champions of the effort. Much more is needed than simply introducing Stratified Policing and/or getting a small group of people to "buy in." Proactive crime reduction will be in direct competition with the ingrained culture of response to calls for service, investigating crimes, and making arrests. Even if people think Stratified Policing makes sense on its surface, this direct competition will inevitably result in some resistance at every level.

Consequently, the agency's executive leadership should articulate Stratified Policing's value and purpose as well as their rationale for change in the context of the agency's culture. The leadership needs to communicate the same message as one voice. They should constantly reinforce the importance of proactive crime reduction, because it takes time to fully integrate Systematic processes and change people's behaviors. This challenge is only overcome by leaders stressing the importance of proactive crime reduction and then holding people accountable for doing what they are supposed to do within the framework.

Accordingly, an accountability process for crime reduction cannot be vague and ambiguous. When this occurs, it is easier for certain individuals to appear as though they are addressing crime problems when they are not. At the same time, this makes it difficult for others to assess whether real progress is being made. In Stratified Policing, accountability is systematic and creates transparency with clear and realistic expectations for both carrying out strategies to reduce crime and accurately assessing results from work being done across the organization.

This process creates an accountability loop that produces incentives at every level, so patrol officers, supervisors, managers, commanders, and executives all play their roles and do their jobs. For example, officers and supervisors work harder at addressing certain crime incidents, so they do not cluster and become crime patterns that are assigned to managers. Patrol managers work harder at holding officers and supervisors accountable for responses to crime patterns so they are not updated with additional crime incidents. Patrol commanders work harder at holding managers accountable for crime pattern responses so they are not updated with additional crimes, so commanders are not held accountable in weekly and monthly agency-wide accountability meetings. These examples clearly illustrate incentives for positive results exist both for people holding others accountable as well as being held accountable themselves.

This accountability loop applies to all immediate, short-, and long-term crime problem processes. It is an extremely important facet of the accountability process that is infused for all proactive work being done. In addition, the accountability loop allows those in leadership positions to engage and reinforce the agency's overall crime reduction goals in a productive way. Importantly, in Stratified Policing accountability for crime reduction is not a negative, or a "gotcha," process. Instead, daily interactions and accountability meetings are collaborative. The accountability process is designed to encourage and enhance a team approach to crime reduction.

We have seen agencies implement accountability meetings where the chief, executive staff, and commanders collaborate to help one another solve issues. In these agencies, individuals do not feel that suggestions, even from their peers, are an attack on their abilities. Rather, they view themselves as a cooperative group attempting to help one another achieve common goals. Obviously, there are times when discussions need to be more direct to provide the necessary pressure and push individuals to achieve certain objectives. However, like any good process, once Stratified Policing is institutionalized, these situations arise less often.

Specifically, two primary objectives of the accountability process are (1) to facilitate and ensure consistent and continual coordination of crime reduction responses, and (2) to evaluate their appropriateness and effectiveness. At each level, accountability processes include real-time accountability of responses, systematic review and documentation in meetings, and evaluation of the impact on crime and disorder. In the chapters on immediate, short-term, and long-term problems, there is a description of accountability and assessment for each problem type.

The purpose of this chapter is to bring all the discrete descriptions together in a more comprehensive discussion of the accountability process. But first, we start by discussing several organizational adjustments and capacities that are important for crime reduction accountability and are often overlooked. We then discuss the entire structure of accountability meetings and effective ways to use evaluation statistics. We close with our final thoughts on Stratified Policing and its implementation.

ORGANIZATIONAL ADJUSTMENTS FOR ACCOUNTABILITY

Since Stratified Policing seeks to infuse systematic proactive crime reduction processes into the existing structure of the police organization, few, if any, major changes need to be made in most agencies. However, there are a few adjustments that support accountability and can accelerate implementation. Although some adjustments are a higher priority than others, they all contribute in the overall implementation for different reasons. These sections provide a discussion of these capabilities that can help streamline crime reduction processes.

Geographic Deployment

Since the community-based approach is integral to crime reduction, the geographic deployment of patrol resources is important. It allows all ranks in patrol to obtain in-depth knowledge of an area within the jurisdiction and build relationships with citizens and community groups. Geographic deployment helps facilitate the ownership of short-term and long-term crime problems by geographic area. Patrol area commanders and their staff are responsible for all problems occurring in their areas across all shifts which streamlines the accountability process so it is more efficient and effective. However, in agencies where geographic deployment is just not possible, at a minimum, we recommend having shift commanders also serve as area commanders (e.g., districts).

Police Data Quality

Crime analysis is central to Stratified Policing. This means that the quality and consistency of police data are very important. In particular, the quality of calls for service, crime reports, and arrest data become a high priority. The proactive crime reduction efforts are identified, prioritized, and evaluated based on these data. Most issues with police data are related to inconsistent, inaccurate, or incomplete entries. Oftentimes these issues are not identified until the data is used for analysis. They are typically unique to an agency's processes for collecting data, but some common examples include inability to distinguish officer- and citizen-generated calls, incorrect addresses, lack of MO information, and inconsistent spelling of names.

Dispatchers, officers, and detectives—as part of their normal duties—are the primary data generators. When issues are found, accountability for ensuring data are collected correctly and consistently lies squarely on the shoulders of supervisors in patrol, investigations, dispatch, and records. However, it is not enough to have officers on one shift or in a specialized unit improve what they do or have records clerks make corrections after the fact. If police data is to be improved, it may require additional training of data collectors, improvements of technology, and enhanced accountability of all supervisors to ensure they are holding their employees accountable.

Crime Analysis Capacity, Technology, and Placement in the Organization

Stratified Policing processes literally start and end with crime analysis, so designated crime analysis personnel are necessary.[1] When possible, we recommend agencies have full-time civilian crime analysts because it is easier to hire individuals who are trained and have chosen crime analysis as their profession. Crime analysts should have the necessary analytical skills to perform at a high level (e.g., no different than a highly trained SWAT operator). In agencies where it is difficult or not possible to hire civilian crime analysts, sworn officers can serve as effective analysts. However, they should be selected based on a skill set needed for the job and be specifically trained to the level necessary to support proactive crime reduction. They also should be assigned full-time to the crime analysis function and not be tasked with other sworn duties.

When possible, we recommend two analysts for an agency with 100 sworn officers and one analyst for every additional 100 officers. Two or more analysts will provide (1) more resources for in-depth analysis of long-term problem offenders, locations, and areas; (2) consistent daily crime pattern analysis (i.e., a second person provides coverage for days off and training);

(3) cross-training and collaboration among the analysts; and (4) an extra layer of review for quality control to ensure relevant and accurate products are disseminated.

In terms of technology, in addition to the agency's CAD, RMS, and law enforcement databases, Microsoft Office and good mapping software serves for most of what crime analysts do for Stratified Policing. In the last twenty years, private companies have developed many specialized statistical and spatial analysis software products for analysts. While some specialized crime analysis programs may be useful, they are not necessary to conduct effective crime analysis. What is most important is that crime analysts create products based on the agency's goals, specific criteria, and community concerns. They should also critically consider other behavioral and environmental factors to create relevant action-oriented and evaluation-oriented products.

Lastly, a very important consideration is the placement of the crime analysis function within the organizational structure. Once an agency begins to systematically use analysis to assign problems and hold personnel accountable, the crime analysts become vulnerable to undue influence by sworn personnel who may seek to manage their own workload and success. This can undermine the accountability process and needs to be avoided. The chief must be confident that the integrity of the processes is not negatively influenced, and the crime analysts must be comfortable being the "voice" and the "truth tellers" for the chief.

Therefore, we strongly recommend placing the crime analyst(s) in the administrative division where no ranks are assigned immediate, short-term, or long-term problems. Crime analysts should be supervised by a commander (i.e., their direct report should be a relatively high rank in the organization) and in a chain of command that reports directly to the chief (e.g., professional standards). The crime analysts do, of course, provide products for patrol, investigations, and other units, but their first responsibility and allegiance are to the chief's crime reduction process.

Stratified Policing Policy and Training

As we have asserted, if proactive crime reduction is to be institutionalized, it should follow the model for what police do for calls-for-service response. A policy is an important part of establishing a practice in a police organization. It dictates what people are supposed to do and makes the roles and responsibilities transparent to everyone in the organization. It also provides a mechanism of accountability (i.e., formal repercussions when the policy is not followed). Police understand the importance of policies since most functions in a police organization have at least one, and some have more than one.

Something as important as reducing crime in the community cannot be vague or optional. So, it follows that crime reduction cannot be institutionalized into an agency until there are written expectations with consequences for not doing the work. We have seen many agencies that do not have a policy outlining specific roles and responsibilities for proactive crime reduction. The common sentiment is that a policy is not needed because crime reduction is part of the job and what police do. If that was true, there would be no need to have any policies related to calls-for-service response, because it is the most fundamental work that police do 24 hours a day, 7 days a week, 365 days a year. But policies do matter and help set the tone that agency leaders are serious about proactive crime reduction. We recommend one comprehensive policy that clearly outlines expectations, roles, and responsibilities for proactive crime reduction. In our work with agencies, their Stratified Policing policies are normally between eight and ten pages. Once the policy is completed, it is treated like all other policies and is disseminated and reviewed by all members of the agency.

As with any implementation of a new process or procedure in a police agency, training is an important step of institutionalizing proactive crime reduction. The training should cover the specific processes for each problem type. It should also cover roles and responsibilities of each rank, unit, division, and bureau as it is outlined in the agency's policy. The training should include a discussion of police culture, evidence-based crime reduction strategies, and the framework of Stratified Policing and its rationale (i.e., what is everyone supposed to do, why, and how). As with any important training (e.g., high liability), a condensed version should be conducted on a continuous basis as part of in-service training. In addition, the FTO/PTO manuals and training should be updated to include work that is done for immediate, short-, and long-term problems by officers.

To help in the implementation process, consideration should be given to the timing of the agency-wide training. We recommend it be done after crime analysis capacity has been established so that the agency is able to produce the necessary crime reduction and accountability analysis products. In addition, the policy should be completed before the training, but only disseminated after the agency-wide training is complete.

Real-Time Accountability Mechanisms

Accountability should be more than a meeting. It is a continual process that occurs in the everyday operations of the organization. For proactive crime reduction to be part of day-to-day missions, it is necessary to capture and track everyday activities as part of the daily accountability. Therefore, we recommend an agency use a real-time communication system to help coordinate and document multifaceted responses occurring at the same time in different areas of a jurisdiction. To accomplish this, we have seen agencies successfully use a variety of intranet platforms, such as Microsoft's SharePoint. This tool serves as the foundation for collecting real-time response and accountability data and aggregating the information to report out in accountability meetings.

An intranet system becomes the hub for tracking responses. It starts with crime analysts posting specific products for short- and long-term crime problems (i.e., similar to dispatching an officer to a call for service). A thread (or discussion board) is created for each problem, and individuals coordinate and input their responses in real time. Supervisors, managers, and commanders responsible for each problem monitor the threads, communicate their expectations for response, and view the ongoing inputs and intelligence collection by officers. Different divisions and units within the police agency share and track their responses in real time as well as report on successes (e.g., problem resolved, arrests made).

Such a system should be designed to also include a reporting function that allows aggregation of all responses implemented by multiple divisions and units for each assigned problem. This information can then be used to report on both individual problems as well as collective efforts for evaluation in accountability meetings. We have found that these types of systems make crime reduction more efficient as well as facilitate people taking the process more seriously. That is, when individuals have to write an account of what they do, they are more deliberate and accurate in their responses. In addition, because this is a transparent forum used by the entire organization, the documentation is taken even more seriously.

A few agencies we have worked with have used the CAD system and GPS for real-time accountability. However, these mechanisms are primarily used for patrol officers and do not easily translate to crime reduction activities.[2] While officers can use CAD to document that they check out at a location to speak to citizens, typically all that is recorded is the time of day, location, and the amount of time spent. It does not track who was contacted or what was accomplished which is important field intelligence. Also, it is very difficult to use these standard police technologies to track proactive activities of detectives, supervisors, managers, and commanders. However, a robust intranet system with GPS can be a powerful tool. It can be used to collect qualitative and quantitative information for real-time intelligence purposes and daily accountability as well as for reporting out in accountability meetings.

STRATIFIED POLICING ACCOUNTABILITY
MEETING STRUCTURE AND EVALUATION

In previous chapters, we touched on how accountability meetings are carried out for immediate, short-, and long-term problems. We thought it was important to integrate the discussions and provide more detail about each type of meeting. For each meeting, this section covers who should lead, be held accountable, and attend. It also covers what should be discussed in each meeting and how crime reduction work is evaluated. Prior to implementing accountability meetings, leaders address the following items, so that the process is more meaningful and realistic and the transition to Stratified Policing accountability is easier:

- Set specific crime reduction goals and their components.
- Set parameters for the identification of each problem type. Set rules for evaluation for success of each problem type.
- Determine ranks that are assigned crime reduction responsibility for each problem type.
- Establish system for documenting, reporting, and aggregating responses.
- Determine the exact nature of the accountability meetings and documentation.

In order to have an accountability process that is consistent and focused on the agency's crime reduction goals, each meeting should have a specific purpose to ensure certain work is being accomplished. In Stratified Policing, every accountability meeting is concise and builds on one another so there is no wasted effort. The accountability system automatically builds in rewards for those who are doing well, and consequences for those who are not.

For example, if a lieutenant is able to quickly resolve a crime pattern by not having any additional crimes (i.e., after 14 days), responses are stopped. The crime pattern would also not be discussed at a higher-level meeting where a captain would be held accountable by an assistant chief. On the other hand, if the same crime pattern is updated with more crimes, the lieutenant would automatically have to continue the responses beyond 14 days. The crime pattern would also be discussed by the patrol captain who would be held accountable in the weekly agency-wide meeting. This system is similar for all immediate, short-, and long-term problems that are assigned.

Expectations for accountability meetings are transparent at the outset, and there are no surprises about what is discussed since problems have already been assigned and responses have started. Therefore, discussion of each problem is succinct and focuses only on the responses implemented since the last meeting (i.e., is not a review of all the responses), and what will be done before the next meeting (i.e., action items). The accountability meetings are characterized by their frequency, purpose, and type of activity they address.

We strongly suggest keeping to the temporal intervals discussed here as we have found these are most realistic and effective—daily, weekly, and monthly. A concrete schedule should be set for these meetings and a clear message that they are mandatory to attend. These meetings should never be optional or simply delegated to a lower rank. We would argue that if crime reduction is important, it warrants its own meeting. These meetings are relatively short and to the point in that they cover crime reduction only and not administrative or personnel issues.

For efficiency, we suggest that during the week the monthly agency-wide meeting is held there be no weekly agency-wide meeting. Once the accountability process has been institutionalized, we have seen various-sized agencies from one to many patrol area commanders all spend around 30 to 60 minutes in their weekly agency-wide meetings and 1 to 3 hours in their monthly meetings. To be efficient and keep the meetings timely, some of the larger agencies (e.g., 10 area commanders) decide to split the weekly agency-wide meetings by region and hold them concurrently (e.g., north/south majors with 5 area commanders each). Some also split the monthly meetings in the same way, and the chief runs them consecutively. This works out to be a total of around 2.5 to 6 hours a month dedicated for agency-wide crime reduction meetings. To ensure the meetings are succinct, we strongly recommend that other organizational information (e.g., review of overtime, holiday, sick leave; status updates from civilian support units; budget information; and personnel decisions) be covered in separate meetings or through written reports.

There is a distinct difference in the purpose of the daily and weekly meetings versus the monthly meeting. Daily and weekly meetings are *action-oriented*, which means that the content and discussion is focused on the coordination of evidence-based responses for the day or upcoming week for immediate, short-term, and long-term problems. In contrast, the monthly meeting facilitates *evaluation-oriented* accountability. They are used to monitor responses and their impact on long-term problems. In addition, they are used to ensure all levels of problems are being addressed appropriately and effectively. They monitor the progress on achieving the agency's crime reduction goals. In this meeting, monthly statistics for each long-term problem as well as each crime reduction goal are discussed.

Daily Briefing

The most important aspect of daily accountability is creating a consistent communication about the crime reduction activities that are to be done each day. Because most agencies already conduct daily roll calls for each patrol shift, this is the first level of accountability meeting. The roll call briefing facilitates action-oriented accountability at the line level between officers, supervisors, and sometimes managers. These are quick conversations that set the tone and reinforce the officer's crime reduction "mission" of the day. These missions include discussions that reinforce responses for short- and long-term problems as determined by the higher ranks assigned responsibility.

Daily roll calls can also be used to mentor and train officers for specific crime reduction related tasks. Because individuals in different areas of the agency (e.g., detectives and specialized units) are required to collaborate and support patrol, they are more active in attending patrol briefings. We have found in agencies that have implemented Stratified Policing, roll call briefings become much more engaging and meaningful to officers because clear proactive crime reduction missions are incorporated.

Weekly Patrol or Investigations Meeting

The weekly patrol or investigations meeting is conducted to ensure that personnel within patrol or the investigations division are held accountable for crime reduction work. In these meetings, commanders (i.e., captains) hold their own managers and, in some cases, supervisors accountable to ensure problems are being addressed appropriately. They also use these meetings to prepare for the weekly agency-wide meeting. The content, organization, and specific attendance are not specified here since its format can be very different by agency and even by commander. These meetings are action-oriented and are used to check in on all immediate, short-term, and long-term problems that have been assigned to those in the commander's chain of command.

Weekly Agency-Wide Meeting

The weekly agency-wide meeting is action-oriented and is a more formal meeting in which multiple units, divisions, and bureaus come together to discuss and collaborate about responses to problems. This meeting is led by a member of the executive staff (e.g., assistant chief). If there is more than one assistant chief, for example, it should be run by the person responsible for patrol operations since patrol is at the center of proactive crime reduction and all other areas support patrol. Patrol commanders discuss repeat incidents and crime patterns that were not adequately resolved based on the agency's set criteria. Progress on significant incidents, problem locations, problem areas, and selected problem offenders are also discussed. The purpose is to bring patrol, investigations, and other division commanders together to ensure responses are being implemented effectively, and units and divisions across the organization are coordinating. Also, this meeting reinforces the idea that resources are shared in order to resolve assigned problems, so the entire agency can meet its crime reduction goals.

Each commander's discussion summarizes the response activity for the previous week and specific action items for the coming week. Assessment is not about generic crime data. It is more precise than that, because it is about specifically measuring commanders' effectiveness of responses to what has been specifically assigned. For example, when a crime pattern is updated with additional crimes, this is a clear indication that the responses are not being effective. This information has already been disseminated by the crime analyst, so everyone is aware of it prior to the meeting.

Lastly, transparency, tracking responses, and knowing what is expected to be accomplished in the upcoming meetings are important facets of the accountability process. We recommend implementing an effective way of tracking what takes place in these meetings. An example is that brief and concise meeting minutes can be taken to capture responses already implemented and action items that should be completed before the next meeting. When efficient tracking is done, the executive running the meeting can use minutes to verify progress on assigned problems and action items each week. During the meeting, additional action items may be added based on what was discussed so that after the meeting, the information is distributed to all commanders as a record of the discussion and final action items for the coming week. The information can then be used to drive the commanders' own weekly meetings as well as help them prepare for the monthly agency-wide meetings.

We have often seen crime analysts tasked to track activity in meetings since they attend, are thoroughly familiar with each problem assigned and its assessment, and are trusted with sensitive data and intelligence information. Whatever an agency chooses to do, we strongly recommend having a clear and succinct process for tracking what responses took place and what actions need to be taken.

Monthly Agency-Wide Meeting

The monthly agency-wide accountability meeting is the chief's meeting. This is where everyone in the agency is held accountable for significant incidents, problem locations, and problem areas, as well as problem offenders. Everyone is also held accountable for crime patterns that are persistent, have not been adequately resolved, and have met the agency's criteria for the commander to discuss in the chief's meeting.

Thus, the meeting sets the tone for the entire agency's crime reduction efforts by holding each rank in respective chains of command accountable for results—evaluation oriented. These meetings are used to discuss crime and disorder statistics that evaluate the progress of responses as well as the agency's crime reduction goals. The chief holds commanders accountable for the effectiveness of responses to individual problems assigned to their command.

Although commanders are directly held accountable in these meetings, executive staff will also be held accountable by the chief for crime reduction activities occurring in their divisions or bureaus. Although extremely rare, there could be a situation where the chief asks a member of the executive staff to answer questions based on how well their own commanders are achieving the agency's crime reduction goals. Importantly, when commanders are not able to attend a meeting, the executive, not the manager, will present on the commander's behalf since the executive is ultimately responsible for all crime reduction under their command. This will avoid commanders simply delegating their responsibilities to lower ranks. While this counters what is traditionally done in accountability meetings, we argue that moving responsibility up the chain-of-command instead of down is more effective and fair.

The discussions in this meeting are more formal than the weekly meetings as technology is typically used to display information and statistics. In each meeting, commanders make succinct presentations that cover the collective work done by various areas of the agency. There are no surprises about what is going to be presented based on what has been assigned and has met the criteria to be discussed. Each commander's presentation contains a brief summary of each problem, responses implemented since last meeting, action items for the coming month, and results for each problem. Here, and in the weekly meeting, lower ranks (managers, supervisors, and officers) should be invited and given the opportunity to attend the meeting. This is a chance to mentor individuals and provide transparency for the entire accountability process.

Finally, in the accountability process, crime analysts, as the "truth tellers," are responsible for creating information that supports the (1) ongoing assessment of the success of short-term problem responses, (2) evaluation of individual long-term problems, and (3) evaluation of the agency's crime reduction goals. Assessment of long-term problem locations and areas is more in depth since these are more complex problems. We cannot recommend clear measures of success since they will depend on the specific nature of the long-term problem addressed. However, evaluation should follow applied research methods in which statistics compare crime and/or disorder levels before and after the responses begin.

Most importantly, evaluation measures come from the data used to identify the problems, so that commanders are held accountable for the activity they have been tasked to address. In addition, success of the responses is evaluated

Figure 10.1. Problem Area Example
Map. Google. (n.d.). Satellite Map. Retrieved February 7, 2020 from URL www.google.com/maps.

based on this activity occurring at the problem location or within the defined boundaries of the problem area. As discussed in chapter 9, Figure 10.1 is a map of an example problem area.

We suggest a straightforward crime analysis product so that evaluation statistics can be systematically prepared and reviewed each month. This chart should be created for both problem locations and problem areas. The product contains the following five components to provide a meaningful, yet succinct, assessment of problem locations and areas:

1. Only the type(s) of crime and/or disorder the patrol manager or commander was tasked to address
2. Monthly counts of activity for 12 months prior to response to account for seasonal variations
3. A demarcation on the chart to indicate when the problem was assigned and responses started
4. Monthly counts of activity after the response
5. Percent change between months of response and same months the previous year

As an example, Figure 10.2 illustrates these components by showing counts for "selected activity" in the problem area from Figure 10.1 for 1 year before and 6 months after the response started. It also includes the percent change from the specific months the response was implemented (i.e., January to June 2021) compared to the same months from the previous year (i.e., January to June 2020).

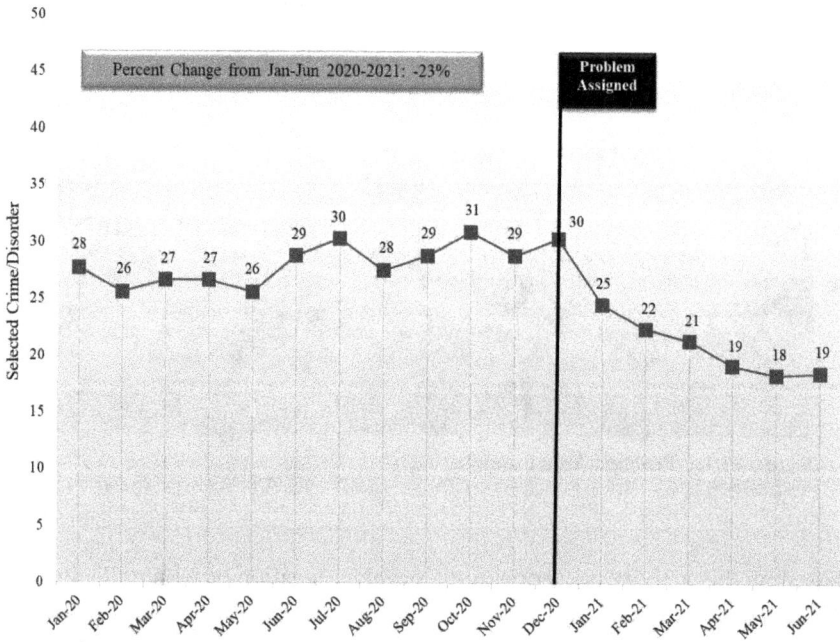

Figure 10.2.   Problem Area Evaluation Chart.

Crime analysts create and then update this chart with the most recent month's crime and a new percent change number. For example in this chart, the percent change compares January through July 2020 to 2021. The charts would be updated until a problem location or problem area is resolved. In addition, to supplement the monthly chart, crime analysts should provide the commanders as well as the chief additional statistics that dig deeper into the data used to evaluate problem locations and problem areas. This breaks down the subsets of crime and disorder to help understand the trends more clearly. For example, the chart would depict the overall activity, but the statistics may show that residential burglary is down but robberies are going up. Patrol commanders are not responsible for putting together their own crime or disorder statistics, so crime analysts provide the chart in electronic format for the commanders to insert directly into in their monthly presentations.

To evaluate the agency's crime reduction goals each month, crime analysts also create products that monitor the agency's crime reduction goals throughout the year. Because goals are set in a particular month and have a set time period, the products should depict the historic counts for the goal, and each month should show the progress toward the goal during the year. Figure 10.3 illustrates a chart we recommend.

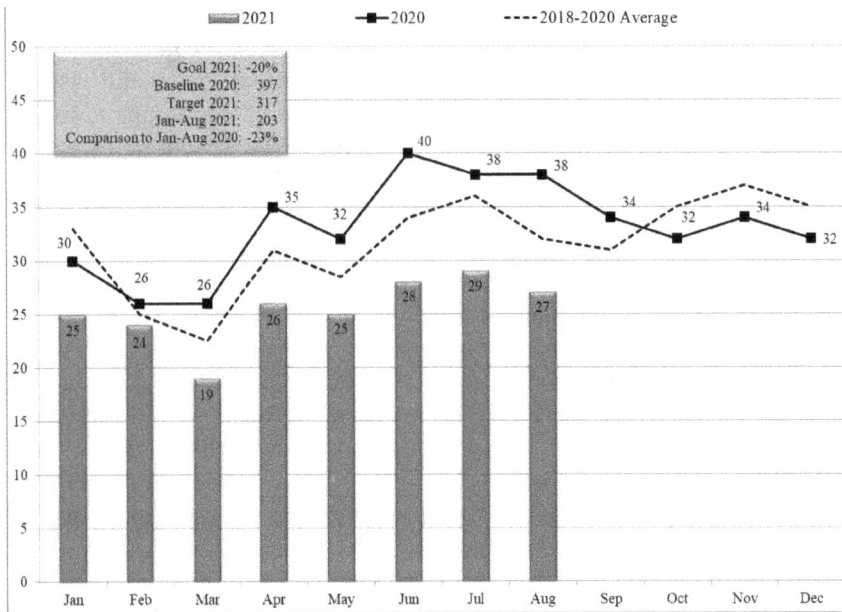

Figure 10.3. Crime Reduction Goal Evaluation Chart. Residential Burglary Goal: 2018 to 2021.

The bars on the chart indicate the ongoing counts of crime for each month in the current year (i.e., goal period). The solid line depicts the monthly counts of the baseline time period (i.e., previous year). The purpose is to give the chief the ability to compare how the agency is currently doing compared to the baseline year. In addition, the dashed line depicts the 3-year average for each month which allows the chief to anticipate the trend in the remaining months of the goal period (i.e., accounting for seasonal variations).

Included on the chart is specific information about the goal and statistics that estimate current progress and comparisons of the year at that point in time. The purpose of these statistics is to monitor whether the agency is on track to meet that particular goal. The following is a description of the statistics in the gray box:

- Goal: Percent decrease restated from goal
- Baseline: Count of activity previous year
- Target: Goal count
- Mon-Mon Current Year: Total for the current year thus far
- Comparison to Mon-Mon Baseline Year: Percent difference from previous year thus far

Thus, Figure 10.3 indicates that with 4 months left in the goal period, the agency is on track to meet the goal since it is 23 percent below the baseline year. For each goal, crime analysts may provide additional information that digs deeper into each goal and seeks to explain the trend a bit more. In this example, crime analysts might find that it is one district that is responsible for more of the decrease than others. They would determine why that is and also discuss whether the other districts are adequately doing their part in meeting the agency's goal. This information would come both from conducting other trend statistics as well as examination of short-term problem results.

This chart and any additional information would be created for each crime reduction goal and updated each month. We recommend that the crime analysts be responsible for presenting this information. Again, crime analysts are the voice of the chief, so the presentation should be focused on what the chief deems important and be succinct. To achieve this, the chief may meet with the crime analysts beforehand to pare down the exact information to include and how it will be discussed in the meeting.

SUMMARY OF ACCOUNTABILITY MEETINGS

Table 10.1 provides an overview of the Stratified Policing accountability structure. It breaks down each meeting and lists who runs the meeting, who is held accountable, the content covered, and other attendees. While these are guidelines and an agency will adjust the structure according to its organizational hierarchy and needs, again, we recommend all levels of meetings are included to achieve the most effective implementation of Stratified Policing.

Table 10.1. Summary of Accountability Meeting Structure

Meeting Type	Who Runs Meeting	Who Is Held Accountable	Content Covered	Other Attendees
Daily	Supervisors	Officers	Mission of the day, share field intelligence for immediate, short-term, and long-term problems, as relevant	Managers, occasionally to ensure meetings are appropriate; investigations and other support personnel, when appropriate
Weekly Patrol or Investigations	Commander	Managers Supervisors	Patrol: Repeat incidents, crime patterns, problem locations/areas Investigations: Significant incidents, problem offenders; coordination with patrol	Officers and detectives, occasionally to be mentored and exposed to the process
Weekly Agency-wide	Executive staff	Commanders	Patrol: Repeat incidents, crime patterns, problem locations/areas Investigations: Significant incidents, problem offenders	Managers; crime analysts; supervisors, officers, detectives, occasionally to be mentored and exposed to the process
Monthly Agency-wide	Chief	Commanders Executive staff	Patrol: Crime patterns, problem locations/areas Investigations: Significant incidents, problem offenders Crime analysts: Evaluation Statistics	All other commanders; managers; crime analysts; supervisors, officers, detectives, occasionally to be mentored and exposed to the process; others as needed

FINAL THOUGHTS

In closing, we provide a few thoughts on implementation and sustainability, both of which should not be taken lightly. While it can be a struggle making any change in a police organization, what Stratified Policing is doing is changing the culture and organizational processes to include systematic agency-wide crime reduction work in a thoughtful way. So, it will take strong leadership and deliberate planning about how the framework fits into the organization and the steps to take for implementation.

There are several factors that can slow down or speed up organizational change. Based on what we have seen, we believe that in a relatively healthy police organization with motivated leaders and a capable crime analysis capacity, full implementation should occur in around 6 months. In terms of sustainability, Stratified Policing is an organizational approach and like any good process, it should be consistently refined so it is as efficient and effective as possible. Similar to the calls-for-service model, Stratified Policing is always a work in progress.

Finally, the police profession has recognized that proactive crime reduction is a worthwhile endeavor, and research shows that there are clear strategies that work. However, police are confronted with the difficult challenge of reducing crime and disorder while increasing community trust. We hope that Stratified Policing provides police a clear and concise solution to these challenges. This book is a culmination of our experiences as practitioners and researchers as well as our partnerships with many different agencies across the United States to implement Stratified Policing and institutionalize crime reduction. Our purpose has been to provide enough detail to understand the rationale behind the structure and processes of Stratified Policing as well as concrete guidance for how to make proactive crime reduction strategies work in the real world of policing. Good luck and stay safe!

NOTES

1. For techniques, examples, and formulas for creating crime analysis products as well as other information on the crime analysis profession, we recommend Santos, R. B. (2017). *Crime analysis with crime mapping.* Thousand Oaks, CA: Sage.

2. Lum, C., Koper, C. S., Wu, X., Johnson, W., and Stoltz, M. (2020). Examining the empirical realities of proactive policing through systematic observations and computer-aided dispatch data. *Police Quarterly*, 1–28. DOI: 10.1177/1098611119896081.

Bibliography

Bernasco, W. (2008). Them again? Same-offender involvement in repeat and near repeat burglaries. *European Journal of Criminology, 5,* 411–31.

Bernasco, W. (2010). A sentimental journey to crime: Effects of residential history on crime location choice. *Criminology, 48*(2), 389–416.

Bernasco, W., and Nieuwbeerta, P. (2005). How do residential burglars select target areas? A new approach to the analysis of criminal location choice. *British Journal of Criminology, 44,* 296–315.

Bichler, G., and Gaines, L. (2005). An examination of police officers' insights into problem identification and problem solving. *Crime and Delinquency, 51*(1), 53–74.

Boba, R., and Santos, R. G. (2011). *A police organizational model for crime reduction: Institutionalizing problem solving, analysis, and accountability.* Washington, DC: Office of Community-Oriented Policing Services.

Braga, A. A., Turchan, B., Papachristos, A. V., and Hureau, D. M. (2019). Hot spots policing of small geographic areas effects on crime. *Campbell Systematic Reviews.* DOI: 10.1002/cl2.1046.

Braga, A., and Weisburd, D. (2012). The effects of focused deterrence strategies on crime: A systematic review and meta-analysis of the empirical evidence. *Journal of Research in Crime and Delinquency, 49*(3), 323–58.

Brantingham, P. J., and Brantingham, P. L. (1982). *Environmental Criminology.* Thousand Oaks, CA: Sage.

Brantingham, P. L., and Brantingham, P. J. (1990). Situational crime prevention in practice. *Canadian Journal of Criminology, 32,* 17–40.

Breul, N., and Keith, M. (2016). Deadly calls and fatal encounters. *National Law Enforcement Memorial Fund.* Retrieved July 31, 2020 from www.nleomf/assets/pdf/officer-safety/Primary-Research-Final-8-2-16.pdf.

Buzawa, E. S., Buzawa, C. G., and Stark, E. D. (2017). *Responding to domestic violence: The integration of criminal justice and human services.* Thousand Oaks, CA: Sage.

Campbell, J. C., Glass, N., Sharps, P. W., Laughon, K., and Bloom, T. (2007). Intimate partner homicide: Review and implications of research and policy. *Trauma, Violence, and Abuse, 8*(3), 246–69.

Campbell, J. C., Messing, J. T., and Williams, K. R. (2017). Prediction of homicide of and by battered women. In J. C. Campbell and J. T. Messing. (Eds.) *Assessing dangerousness: Domestic violence offenders and child abusers.* New York: Springer Publishing Company.

Center for Problem-Oriented Policing. (2020). https://popcenter.asu.edu/.

Chainey, S. P., Curtis-Ham, S. J., Evans, R. M., and Burns, G. J. (2018). Examining the extent to which repeat and near repeat patterns can prevent crime. *Policing: An International Journal, 41*(5), 608–22.

Clarke, R. V. (1980). Situational crime prevention: Theory and practice. *British Journal of Criminology, 20,* 136–47.

Clarke, R. V. (Ed.) (1997). *Situational crime prevention: Successful case studies* (2nd ed.). New York: Harrow and Heston.

Clarke, R. V., and Eck, J. (2005). *Crime analysis for problem solvers: In 60 small steps.* Washington, DC: Office of Community-Oriented Policing Services.

Clarke, R. V., and Weisburd, D. (1994). Diffusion of crime control benefits: Observations on the reverse of displacement. In R. V. Clarke. (Ed.) *Crime prevention studies* (vol. 2, pp. 165–83). Monsey, NY: Criminal Justice Press.

Cohen, L., and Felson, M. (1979). Social change and crime rate trends: A routine activity approach. *American Sociological Review, 44*(4), 588–608.

Cordner, G. W. (2014). Community policing. In M. Reisig and R. Kane. (Eds.) *The Oxford handbook of police and policing* (pp. 148–71). New York: Oxford University Press.

Cordner, G. W., and Biebel, E. (2005). Problem-oriented policing in practice. *Criminology and Public Policy, 4*(2), 155–80.

Coupe, T., and Blake, L. (2006). Daylight and darkness targeting strategies and the risks of being seen at residential burglaries. *Criminology, 44,* 431–64.

Dabney, D. (2010). Observations regarding key operational realities in a Compstat model of policing. *Justice Quarterly, 27,* 28–51.

Eck, J., and Spelman, W. (1987). *Problem solving: Problem-oriented policing in Newport News.* Washington, DC: Police Executive Research Forum.

Famega, C. N. (2005). Variation in officer downtime: A review of the research. *Policing: An International Journal of Police Strategy and Management, 28*(3), 388–414.

Famega, C. N., Frank, J., and Mazerolle, L. (2005). Managing police patrol time: The role of supervisor directives. *Justice Quarterly, 22*(4), 540–59.

Farrell, G., and Pease, K. (1993). *Once bitten, twice bitten: Repeat victimization and its implications for crime prevention* (Crime Prevention Unit Series Paper 46). London: Home Office, Police Research Group.

Felson, M., and Boba, R. (2010). *Crime and everyday life.* Thousand Oaks, CA: Sage.

Felson, M., and Clarke, R. V. (1998). *Opportunity makes the thief: Practical theory for crime prevention* (Police Research Series Paper 98). London: Home Office, Research, Development and Statistics Directorate, Policing and Reducing Crime Unit.

Friday, P., Lord, V., Exum, M., and Hartman, J. (2006). *Evaluating the impact of a specialized domestic violence police unit* (Final Report No. NCJ 215916). https://www.ncjrs.gov/pdffiles1/nij/grants/215916.pdf.

Gill, C., Weisburd, D. L., Telep, C. W., Vitter, Z., and Bennett, T. (2014). Community-oriented policing to reduce crime, disorder and fear and increase satisfaction and legitimacy among citizens: A systematic review. *Journal of Experimental Criminology, 10*(4), 399–428.

Goldstein, H. (1990). *Problem-oriented policing.* New York: McGraw-Hill.

Graves, K. N., Hunt, E. D., Sumner, M., Casterline, L., Fluegge, L., Varner, L., et al. (2011). *Applying a focused deterrence approach to domestic violence.* Greensboro: Center for Youth, Family, and Community Partnerships, University of North Carolina at Greensboro.

Groff, E. R., Ratcliffe, J. H., Haberman, C. P., Sorg, E. T., Joyce, N. M., and Taylor, R. B. (2015). Does what police do at hot spots matter? The Philadelphia policing tactics experiment. *Criminology, 53*(1), 23–53.

Grove, L. E., Farrell, G., Farrington D. P., and Johnson, S. D. (2012). *Preventing repeat victimisation: A systematic review.* Stockholm: Bra—The Swedish National Council for Crime Prevention.

Hirschel, D. (2008). Domestic violence cases: What research shows about arrest and dual arrest rates (NIJ ePub). Retrieved July 31, 2020 from https://www.ncjrs.gov/App/Publications/abstract.aspx?ID=244581.

Hirschel, D., Buzawa, E., Pattavina, A., and Faggiani, D. (2007). Domestic violence and mandatory arrest laws: To what extent do they influence police arrest decisions? *Journal of Criminal Law and Criminology, 98,* 255–98.

Houston, C. (2014). How feminist theory became (criminal) law: Tracing the path to mandatory criminal intervention in domestic violence cases. *Michigan Journal of Gender and Law, 21*(2), 217–72.

Johnson, S. D., and Bowers, K. J. (2004). The burglary as a clue to the future: The beginnings of prospective hot-spotting. *European Journal of Criminology, 1,* 237–55.

Johnson, S. D., Bowers, K. J., and Pease, K. (2012). Towards the modest predictability of daily burglary counts. *Policing, 6*(2), 167–76.

Johnson, S. D., Guerette, R. T., and Bowers, K. (2014). Crime displacement: What we know, what we don't know, and what it means for crime reduction. *Journal of Experimental Criminology, 10*(4), 549–71.

Johnson, S. D., Lab, S., and Bowers, K. J. (2008). Stable and fluid hot spots of crime: Differentiation and identification. *Built Environment, 34*(1), 32–46.

Johnson, S. D., and Summers, L. (2015). Testing ecological theories of offender spatial decision making using a discrete choice model. *Crime and Delinquency, 61*(3), 454–80.

Johnson, S. D., Summers, L., and Pease, K. (2007). *Vehicle crime: Communicating spatial and temporal patterns.* London: Jill Dando Institute of Crime Science.

Johnson, S. D., Summers, L., and Pease, K. (2009). Offenders as forager: A direct test of the boost account of victimization. *Journal of Quantitative Criminology, 25,* 181–200.

Klein, A. R. (2009). *Practical implications of current domestic violence research: For law enforcement, prosecutors, and judges.* Washington, DC: US Department of Justice, National Institute of Justice.

Koper, C. S. (1995). Just enough police presence: Reducing crime and disorderly behavior by optimizing patrol time in crime hot spots. *Justice Quarterly*, 12, 649–72.

Lum, C., Koper, C. S., Wu, X., Johnson, W., and Stoltz, M. (2020). Examining the empirical realities of proactive policing through systematic observations and computer-aided dispatch data. *Police Quarterly*, 1–28. DOI: 10.1177/1098611119896081.

McLaughlin, L., Johnson, S. D., Bowers, K. J., Birks, D. J., and Pease, K. (2006). Police perceptions of the long- and short-term spatial distribution of residential burglary. *International Journal of Police Science and Management*, 9(2), 99–111.

Office of Community-Oriented Policing Resource Center. https://cops.usdoj.gov/ric/ric.php.

Police Executive Research Forum [PERF]. (2015). Police improve response to domestic violence, but abuse often remains the "hidden crime." *Subject to Debate, 29 (1),* January/February. Retrieved July 31, 2020 from http://www.policeforum.org/assests/docs/Subject_to_Debate/Debate2015/debate_2015_janfeb.pdf.

Ratcliffe, J. H., and McCullagh, M. (2001). Chasing ghosts? Police perception of high crime areas. *British Journal of Criminology*, 41, 330–41.

Santos, R. B. (2014). The effectiveness of crime analysis for crime reduction: Cure or diagnosis? *Journal of Contemporary Criminal Justice, 30*(2), 147–68.

Santos, R. B. (2017). *Crime analysis with crime mapping.* Thousand Oaks, CA: Sage.

Santos, R. B., and Santos, R. G. (2015). Examination of police dosage in residential burglary and theft from vehicle micro-time hot spots. *Crime Science, 4*(27), 1–12.

Santos, R. B., and Santos, R. G. (2016). Offender-focused police strategies in residential burglary and theft from vehicle hot spots: A partially blocked randomized controlled trial. *Journal of Experimental Criminology, 12*(3), 373–402.

Santos, R. B., and Santos, R. G. (2020). Proactive police response in property crime micro-time hot spots: Results from a partially-blocked blind random control trial. *Journal of Quantitative Criminology*, 1–21. DOI 10.1007/s10940-020-09456-8.

Santos, R. B., and Taylor, B. (2014). The integration of crime analysis into police patrol work: Results from a national survey of law enforcement. *Policing: An International Journal of Police Strategies and Management, 37*(3), 501–20.

Santos, R. G. (February 2011). Systematic pattern response strategy: Protecting the beehive. *FBI Law Enforcement Bulletin.* https://leb.fbi.gov/2011/february/systematic-pattern-response-strategy-protecting-the-beehive.

Santos, R. G. (2018). Offender and family member perceptions after an offender-focused hot spots policing strategy. *Policing: An International Journal, 41*(3), 386–400.

Santos, R. G. (2018). Police organizational change after implementing crime analysis and evidence-based strategies through stratified policing. *Policing: A Journal of Policy and Practice, 12*(3), 288–302.

Santos, R. G., and Santos, R. B. (2015). An ex post facto evaluation of tactical police response in residential theft from vehicle micro-time hot spots. *Journal of Quantitative Criminology, 31*(4), 679–98.

Santos, R. G., and Santos, R. B. (2015). Practice-based research: Ex post facto evaluation of evidence-based police practices implemented in residential burglary micro-time hot spots. *Evaluation Review, 39*(5), 451–79.

Science, M., Johnstone, J., Roth, D. E., Guyatt, G., and Loeb, M. (2012). Zinc for the treatment of the common cold: A systematic review and meta-analysis of randomized controlled trials. *Canadian Medical Journal, 184*(10), 551–61.

Scott, M. (2010). Evaluating the effectiveness of problem-oriented policing. *Criminology and Public Policy, 9*(1), 135–37.

Sechrist, S. M., and Weil, J. D. (2018). Assessing the impact of a focused deterrence strategy to combat intimate partner domestic violence. *Violence against Women, 24*, 243–65.

Shah, S., Burch, J., and Neusteter, S. R. (2018). *Leveraging CompStat to include community measures in police performance management. Perspectives from the field.* New York: Vera Institute of Justice.

Sherman, L. W. (1990). Police crackdowns: Initial and residual deterrence. *Crime and Justice, 12*, 1–48.

Skogan, W. G. (2019). Advocate: Community policing. In D. L. Weisburd and A. A. Braga. (Eds.) *Police innovation: Contrasting perspectives* (pp. 27–44). New York: Cambridge University Press.

Sullivan, C. M. (2005). Interventions to address intimate partner violence: The current state of the field. In J. R. Lutzker. (Ed.) *Preventing violence: Research and evidence-based intervention strategies* (pp. 195–212). Atlanta: Centers for Disease Control and Prevention.

Telep, C. W., and Weisburd, D. (2012). What is known about the effectiveness of police practices in reducing crime and disorder? *Police Quarterly, 15*(4), 331–57.

Townsley, M., Homel, R., and Chaseling, J. (2003). Infectious burglaries: A test of the near repeat hypothesis. *British Journal of Criminology, 43*, 615–33.

Wallace, D., Papachristos, A. V., Meares, T., and Fagan, J. (2016). Desistance and legitimacy: The impact of offender notification meetings on recidivism among high risk offenders. *Justice Quarterly, 33*(7), 1237–64.

Weisburd, D. (2015). The law of crime concentration and the criminology of place. *Criminology, 53*(2), 133–57.

Weisburd, D., and Majmundar, M. K. (Eds.) (2018). *Proactive policing: Effects on crime and communities.* Washington, DC: The National Academies Press.

Weisburd, D., Mastrofski, S. D., McNally, A. M., Greenspan, R., and Willis, J. J. (2003). Reforming to preserve: Compstat and strategic problem solving in American policing. *Criminology and Public Policy, 2*, 421–56.

Weisburd, D., Telep, C. W., Hinkle, J. C., and Eck, J. (2010). Is problem-oriented policing effective in reducing crime and disorder? Findings from a Campbell systematic review. *Criminology and Public Policy, 9*(1), 139–72.

Willis, J. J., Mastrofski, S. D., and Kochel, T. R. (2010). The co-implementation of CompStat and community policing. *Journal of Criminal Justice, 38*, 969–80.

Index

About the Authors

Roberto Santos is an associate professor of criminal justice and codirector of the Center for Police Practice, Policy and Research at Radford University in Radford, Virginia. He retired after 22 years from the Port St. Lucie, Florida Police Department where he worked in, supervised, and commanded every division within the agency. He is a graduate of the FBI National Academy (Class 239). Prior to policing, Dr. Santos was a sergeant in the Marine Corps and is a veteran of Desert Storm/Desert Shield. Dr. Santos is recognized nationally and internationally for his impact on the field of policing through his high-level rigorous research, translation of research to practice, and hands on work with police organizations. As codirector of the Center for Police Practice, Policy, and Research, Dr. Santos shares in the administration of the Center and management of large-level, grant-funded research projects. The purpose of the Center is to facilitate collaboration among researchers and police practitioners to foster a unique blend of evidence-based and practice-based police policy and research. He has served as a subject matter expert for the federal agencies (Office of Community-Oriented Policing Services and Bureau of Justice Assistance) and State governments (Maryland, Virginia, and Delaware) as well as police research organizations, such as the Institute for Intergovernmental Research, the Police Executive Research Forum, the International Association of Chiefs of Police, and the National Police Foundation. He conducts assessments, evaluation, training and technical assistance for local police departments, county sheriff's offices, and state police across the United States where he works closely with leadership as well as operational personnel to integrate policies and best practices into day-to-day police operations. Dr. Santos earned his master of science in criminology and criminal justice from Florida Atlantic University and his doctor of philosophy in criminal justice with a concentration in organizational leadership from Nova Southeastern University.

Rachel Santos is a professor of criminal justice and codirector of the Center for Police Practice, Policy and Research at Radford University in Radford, Virginia. Dr. Santos has been working with police organizations since 1994 and conducts practice-based research on organizational change and accountability, crime analysis, and sustainability of evidence-based crime reduction strategies in police organizations. Dr. Santos started her career as a crime analyst for the Tempe, Arizona, Police Department then served as a senior research associate and director of the Crime Mapping Laboratory at the National Police Foundation in Washington, DC. Currently, as a codirector of the Center for Police Practice, Policy, and Research, Dr. Santos shares in the administration of the Center and manages large-level, grant-funded research projects that focus on identifying and testing practical police strategies. She conducts assessments, training, and technical assistance for local police departments, county sheriff's offices, and state police and serves as subject matter expert for large-level federal initiatives. Dr. Santos is an international expert on crime analysis and its role in effective crime reduction and has conducted experimental research and evaluation of police practices. She has published many final reports, practitioner guidebooks, book chapters, and articles for both academic and professional journals. She has one of the only sole authored books on crime analysis in its fourth edition, *Crime Analysis with Crime Mapping*. Dr. Santos earned her master of arts and doctor of philosophy in sociology from Arizona State University.

www.ingramcontent.com/pod-product-compliance
Lightning Source LLC
Chambersburg PA
CBHW050519280326
41932CB00014B/2374